LESSONS
of
COUNSELLING

BHARAT B. GUPTA

Published by

Notion Press Media Pvt. Ltd.

This book is dedicated to the numerous teachers and students who have left an indelible mark on our lives, shaping the thoughts expressed and conveyed within these pages. A special recognition and appreciation to the team of Vidya Vahini, who has taught me the winning ways of Education.

Bharat B Gupta

FOREWORD

It has never been harder for young adults to live by the values they may have been raised with, while keeping up with the pressures from their peers, media and society. Conflicting expectations of themselves and from those around them, can stress them out and confuse them, leading to unhappiness, low self- esteem and to choices which may offer a temporary escape from their angst but cause ruin in the long term.

Access to a good counsellor can make all the difference in the life of a confused Teen or Tween, and I believe every person in need of emotional and spiritual support should have access to one. Universal teacher to humanity, Bhagawan Sri Sathya Sai Baba has raised and guided thousands of His students personally through such dilemmas during His sojourn on earth. He has also graciously shared His wisdom and insights with His staff and through His writings so that His mission may go on smoothly even in His physical absence. Access to this repository of tried, tested and true guidance can make or restore a young life, save a family from losing a precious child to undue pressure and reinforce confidence and faith in the distressed young adults.

I congratulate the vision and leadership of Sri B.B. Gupta and his team at DCM Group of Schools, Chandigarh, recognized the need to empower High School teachers in this direction so that they may have access to well-researched and systematically planned material that can be used by educators everywhere to fulfil this counselling need in their learning communities. As part of the Sri Sathya Sai Vidya Vahini, Sri B.B. Gupta and his team at DCM Group of Schools, Chandigarh, have always supported the program that blends the eternal values of an ancient civilization within our learnings. The need for highlighting the lasting and meaningful goals of life has never been greater and this book is an offering in that direction.

It is a matter of great joy and satisfaction that we will be placing this composition of counselling lessons as a handy booklet for teachers at the lotus feet of our Sadguru, Bhagawan Sri Sathya Sai Baba at Prasanthi Nilayam on December 1, 2018 on the occasion of the SSSVV Annual Meet. We pray that it may reach the hands of every teacher in this great nation of Bharat and beyond, who in turn will harness Bhagawan's wisdom to empower younger generations with self-confidence and strengthen their faith in the unchanging values of Truth, Right Conduct, Peace, Non-violence and Love in an ever changing world.

Karuna Munshi
Director, Sri Sathya Sai Vidya Vahini

ACKNOWLEDGEMENTS

This book owes its origin to innumerable discussions with my staff, students and friends and to the learnings I had from Sri Sathya Sai Vidya Vahini. There are too many to mention individually by name, but to them all, I offer my thanks for their part in consolidating my thoughts on the various lessons of this book. Their continuous encouraging suggestions and augmentation of my ideas are reflected in this entire book. All the inspirations are the blessings of my divine mentor Sri Sathya Sai Bhagwan, who has always held my hand to pen the words in this book.

This book was able to take this shape with the guidance of my mentor Dr. Art-ong Jumsai Na Ayudhya, Chief Administrator of Sathya Sai School, Lopburi province (Thailand) and I am deeply indebted to him.

I am grateful to Mr. Raj Kumar Jain, Ms. Vishali Kaushal, Ms. Sangeeta Tripathi, Ms. Arti Sharma, Dr. K.C. Jindal, Mr. Ram Bhardwaj and Mrs. Mohini Madaan for their constant encouragement and creation of Assets as per Vidya Vahini concepts. Their convincing inducements have helped me a lot to write "Lessons of Counselling".

Last, but by no means least, my sincere thanks are due to my patient wife Ms. Usha Gupta, Principal, DC Model School, who has spared a lot of my time which was, perhaps, hers. Her contribution to this book extends far beyond being just a source of inspiration.

Bharat B. Gupta

C O N T E N T S

DAY 0
Guidelines for the Teachers

Dear Teachers,

The lessons in your hand will serve as guidelines and include topics chosen for guidance and counselling of the students of Classes 9th and 10th.These lessons are not meant for all students, but are specifically meant for the students who have become disoriented, have become victims of inferiority complex and have lost their self-confidence. Such students may think that they cannot compete with others or their capacity to comprehend is not equal to others. While conducting a Class (using these lessons), you must make an effort to win their trust. There is no need to be in haste. Make the lesson interactive instead of sticking to the conventional lecture method. Explain your viewpoint with the help of some activities. This process may take some extra time but will be well worth it. Develop self-confidence in students by conducting ice-breaking sessions. Create a conducive environment and win their trust so that they may open up to share their personal problems with you without feeling uncomfortable. Once the barriers are broken, they will end up learning more than what you are teaching. Never betray their trust under any circumstances. Difference in opinion should be respected and acknowledged. Such a discussion will be more fruitful and will yield quicker and better results. If you feel that a student is right in logic or facts, accept him, modify your script or convince him with your rationale. Do not expect immediate answers to your questions. Give the students some time to think over the problem. Once they have identified the key issue, your job is almost over.

Ultimate objective of the entire exercise is to make them indulge in self-diagnosis and develop confidence that they can overcome their inner devils of inferiority complex. Please feel free to plan the lessons as per your convenience, keeping in view that you have to reach out to the children in the best possible way. There is no need to try and cover the complete lesson in a day. You may assign them some homework but it should be either self-diagnostic or introspective in nature.

Try to put yourself in the place of the children and think about the planning of each lesson. You cannot get away by just saying, 'It is because IT IS'. You will have to give some logical reasons for what you say or preach. Find out activities relevant to your topic so as to make the concepts reach their heart and not just the head. These lessons should not be an academic burden on them. Rather, these are meant to play a vital role to infuse enthusiasm in their life. These lessons should guide them about the art of maintaining balance between materialism and spiritualism, which is the supreme need of the hour.

The first asset i.e. the **'Main Script'** of the lesson is being decorated by SIX more ASSETS. The purpose of adding these assets is to make the process of imparting education insightful, inspiring, enjoyable and participative. The role of each asset is different but still, these are not like water tight compartments. Neither their order, nor their purpose is fixed. Which asset should be picked up and applied first, depends on the nature of the lesson. I will try to amplify the role of each asset to you. A lesson which is the 'Main' Script (MS) is like the lesson of the syllabus, the objective of which is pre-defined. Every lesson has some important message to convey to the teens. Here, the purpose is to educate them not to cross the 'Laxman Rekha', when they grow. This 'Laxman Rekha' which consists of five major values, is meant to save the child from the glare of worldly attractions which if used judiciously, may help the child to become more inspired, but if overused, may just spoil their career.

The second asset is **'Inquisitive Questions'**. Usually inquisitive questions are used to start the lesson. It is not 'P.K. testing' like we used to do in B.Ed. The purpose here is to create interest in the child about the lesson and bring in a sense of curiosity. It is used as an ice breaker too. Then comes **'Suggested Activity'** (SA). Sometimes SA is used to introduce the lesson. It is a good tool for a category of children who learn better by doing. It also promotes participation. The fourth asset is **'Day to Day Relevance'** (D2D). The role of D2D is to motivate a child and to convince him or her as to how the content being imparted, is going to be useful in their daily life. For a student, it is important to know the utility of each lesson in their day to day life. Then comes **'Interesting Asides'** asset (IA). Role of IA is to make the lesson enjoyable. To retain their interest in the lesson, add some interesting asides to the main script. By adding history, map, location, when, how etc. about the lesson, a greater sense of interest is developed in the child's mind. It can be a joke too. The idea is to bring a smile on the face of the child. It may not be directly related to the academic part. Next asset is **'Value Content'** (VC). Role of a VC is to inspire the child and to make the child GOOD too. In fact VC is a very important tool to make 'education for life (and not just for living)'. Seventh and last but not the least asset is the **'Questions to Assess'**. Its role is to see how well the 'learning' has taken place. It is a test for teachers as well. If after practicing this book in your school, you want to serve others too, please do not hesitate to mail your feedback to bbgupta.sssvv@gmail.com so that your services for the 'society' may be availed. Sometimes, it is not possible to check your own mistake while the other can easily detect the same.

Though now our government is trying to change the pattern, but our education system as of now is designed more for living than for life. It has been so since the British period, because the British wanted people who had factual knowledge, could read and write, and who could serve their purpose of clerical work. All they wanted was a person who may type their letters in correct English or may be good with memory and cramming. Even after the Brits left our country, we continued to follow the same pattern. The practical and application aspect of Education is missing.

Present state of education needs to be changed. Our education system lacks practical application. Very little knowledge is applied after getting the Degree. There is not much difference between the weak and the intelligent. The intelligent vomits out whatever he has mugged up after the exam and the weak vomits out everything before the exam. An M.Sc. in Physics is unable to fix a tripped fuse in his own house. An M.Sc. in Botany does not know the benefits of a Tulsi plant. An M.A. in English is unable to draft his own application. Children in the nursery repeat the same "Baa Baa black sheep" or "Johny Johny Yes Papa". Even today we depend on question papers of last ten years as if nothing new is possible. Weightage is given to marks and not remarks. Nothing much is considered about patriotism. Simply at the end of the lecture, the teacher writes the answer on the black board which the students copy, and subsequently reproduce it during the exam. If they have good memory, they may even secure above 90% marks. Thank GOD, now our attention is gradually focusing on HOT (High Order Thinking) questions. We need to change the mind set of children as well as parents. Even now, you will find 'financer' parents, who feel that one tuition in Mathematics can get his child 40% and by keeping two tuitions, his child would get 80%.

Let us now visualize the problem of education. This lesson is kept for teachers only so that the objective of 'counselling' may be clear to them. What is the purpose of education? "End of Education is Character" says Sri Sathya Sai Baba. If education is not leading towards character building, there is no use of such education. We are to prepare our young generation for life and not for mere living. So let us now understand the difference between living and life.

Education is not just for giving information only, it is meant for TRANSFORMATION of a child. It is not for securing marks only, it is meant for REMARKS. There is a need to teach through HEART instead of teaching through HEAD alone. Once an Indian Professor went to Russia to deliver some lectures to Russian students. He thought of a plan. He got a tape recorder and recorded all his lessons, went to the lecture room and switched his Tape Recorder on. After finishing his first lecture, he explained the procedure to his Assistant and went away. The Assistant was supposed to put on the tape recorder so that the Professor might get time to enjoy Russia. This procedure went on for 2-3 days. After that the Assistant would just put on the Tape Recorder and leave the room. After a week, when the professor went to check his Class, he saw a tape recorder on each bench. The tape recorder was delivering the lesson and from each bench, a tape recorder was 'listening'. There was no student in the Class. So if the Tape Recorder is to speak, a tape recorder would listen. If a teacher is to use his mind, children will also use their mind only. Teachers are the role models for children. As is the tank, so will be the tap.

The ultimate objective of these lessons is to motivate the children. We are to make them optimistic. We are to ask them to get rid of their past and to start living in the present. There will hardly be any person who does not have even a single 'devil' in him/her. But the game is to accept the person as he or she is. This is just like a Card Player, who does not ask for a change in cards just because his cards are not good enough. Rather, he plays the game with the cards he has in hand but with a different application of mind. These lessons are meant to generate interaction, and you just cannot accept things in the traditional way, as we have been habitual till now. You are to add lots of love and patience to the existing soup. Do proper reading before going to class and plan the strategy beforehand. Children are going to have some unpredictable questions too. You make a rule that the answer will be given the next day. Love is the biggest weapon. In senior classes, even the love is not provided. We are to go systematically and give them love, if still there is no change, just double the dose of love. You are to calculate the input you are giving and the output we get out of the whole exercise. You are to put your 100% if you want to have an impact on these children. God has given you a task to accomplish.

Assets :

Inquisitive Questions
1) Why is there a difference in the achievement levels of children?
2) Who is responsible for the difference in the achievement levels of the children?
3) Do you think that only the verbal instructions will result in any transformation?
4) If there is a transformation, who can be considered more effective – the teacher or the lesson? Why?
5) What is the difference between our education system and the education system abroad, and why is this difference?

Suggestive Activity
Read this book thoroughly and plan the yearly calendar.
Discuss your plan with your Principal.

Interesting Asides
When you listen to any lecture, chances of retention are 15%. If you use any teaching aids, the chances of retention go up to 40%. But if the students learn through doing an activity (ears, eyes and hands), then the chances of retention may rise up to 95%. There may be some doubt about the transformation of children but there will definitely be a change in the attitude of the teacher.

Day to Day Relevance
Teaching can be done by two methods; one is head to head - it is for our examination system and makes a person great. Another form of teaching is done from heart to heart - it is for transformation, it makes a person GOOD also.

Value Content

As is the tank so will the tap be.

Education is for life and not for merely living only.

Questions to Assess

1) Which out of the two - good and great, has a higher priority and why?
2) It is said that you cannot change others. The maximum you can do is to change yourself, then why are we making efforts to change the children?
3) If there is a transformation, what would be the main factor – 'role model' aspect of the teacher or 'effectiveness' of the lesson?
4) Do you think this counselling lesson is every one's cup of tea, or there should be something special in a teacher. If yes, what is that special attribute?
5) Go through the lessons. Do you agree with the sequence of lessons?
6) What will be the impact when education will be for life (HOT)?

Day 1
The Beginning

Dear Children,

Today is our very first day. Before we start our Class, let us pray to God, who is supreme, invincible and omnipotent, to bless our souls with refinement of thoughts and guide us to realise the objective of this Class. The main objective is to raise the level of efficiency of every child and to bring everyone at par with high rank children. Let us pray to GOD that these classes may bring positive changes in your life even though most of you may be going through a rough phase of life at present and feeling hopeless at the same time. Many of you may be feeling that you have caused irreparable loss to yourself and nothing can compensate now. Some of you may feel that the syllabus taught in the class is beyond your comprehension and it looks as if the curriculum taught is of some different dimension. As soon as you open your books, you start feeling drowsy and lose interest. Many of you may feel that it is hard to concentrate in the class and to listen to the teachers' talks attentively. Even if you try hard and learn some content, you tend to forget it quite soon. Many of you might have developed the tendency of befooling your parents by socialising through gadgets, on the pretext of studying. Some of you may have fallen into bad company resulting in indulging in unfair practices. Many of you must have realised the root cause of this problem i.e. bad company of friends but now you might be finding it hard to come out of it or to part from your friends. You might have got addicted to the technology to the extent that now your virtual world is dominating your real world. These gadgets have become an integral part of your routine life and you find it difficult to live without them. Due to inappropriate exposure, many of you may have started indulging in adult practices. Some may yet be day dreaming and whenever they find leisure time they may be having a dream of their photo on the first page in the leading newspapers. When you do not care about time, a day comes when time proves its worth. One must respect time if one wants to be respected by others.

If you think deeply, whom do you see responsible for this condition? Are these the ones whom you hold so close to your hearts i.e. your friends? Or do you hold your parents, who have always been over demanding, responsible for this condition? Are there some people who are associated with you in one way or the other? I understand that there must be many frustrations building up in your mind, resulting in angry outbursts, or other negative thoughts. You might be holding your siblings responsible for your present condition. The probable reason might be the comparison made by your parents. It may be provoking you resulting in a revengeful feeling and frustration.

Instead of carrying grudges inside your hearts, you should always forgive and forget. Forgive the people, forget the bitter experiences and move ahead in life with a better plan for the future. The most important requirement for self-improvement is to live in the present. Close your eyes and think again about your aim in life. Are you prepared to achieve your aim? What is your action plan? What are the hurdles in your way of executing your action plan? Can you manage to achieve your aim of life with your present ways of working? Doesn't your conscience insist that you should put in more effort? Don't you think that you need to modify your ways to achieve the heights that you dream of? What kind of positivity is required to minimize the effect of negativity?

Activity:
Prepare a list of negative traits that you should overcome to fulfil your aim in life. On the other side, prepare a list of the positive traits that you should develop in yourself. Rationalization is required. There is no free lunch. We will have to pay the price. Are you ready to pay the price? All your well-wishers are waiting for you to come out with strong positivity.

There is no best time to start a good thing. The time is now. Let us start working upon ourselves and show the world that YOU CAN DO IT.

Let me tell you that you are the fortunate few whom God has chosen for special blessings. At this point of time, you may be finding it hard to believe because you think that the time has gone by and cannot be retrieved.

Let us contemplate deeper into it because 'Picture Abhi Baaki Hai Mere Dost.....'

My first answer to all your questions is – Yes, it is never too late provided you put in a little effort from your side with a strong will power to bring out the change in yourself and leave the rest to God. The foremost thing is to have faith in Him. Only indulging in daydreaming will not solve the problems. The past is gone. The future is beyond your reach. But the present is in your hands and you need to utilize it with full wisdom. With great determination and perseverance, you can make your dreams into reality. To begin with, we need to adhere to the 4F formula. i.e. **F**ollow the Master, **F**ace the Devil, **F**ight till the End and **F**inish the game. Before going to bed tonight, just ask yourself if you actually want to finish the game? If you want to excel, only one person can hamper your game, and that is you only. Its vice versa is also true.

I believe that each one of you wants to come out of the swamp that you are stuck in. But you need to think deeply about the challenges that you may face in this journey of self- improvement. It is the time for self-awakening. Don't ponder over your past. Keeping firm faith in your Master will help you in bringing the desired change in your life. You have to mainly follow two Chief Masters. The first one is your Mentor and the second is your own conscience to whom you are answerable. Take it as a challenge. Many of you might have faced certain terminology that is used frequently by your acquaintances i.e.

Low IQ, lack of intelligence, 'duffer', and so on. Let these words not affect you anymore. You prove with your efforts how misfit these 'adjectives' are for us.

Just tell yourself only two magic words, i.e. **'I WILL'**. Low IQ is nothing but merely a block in our mind. You need to overcome it with the strength of your positivity.

Visualisation:

Think that your Class 10th result has been declared and all teachers are praising you. They are awestruck while going through your marksheet as you have scored much beyond their expectations and generalisations. Before going to bed tonight, tell yourself that you can do it. Have a conversation with God that you are His child and that you deserve all the right to succeed just as others do.

Assets :

Inquisitive Questions

1) What do you mean by the word distraction?
2) Name a few things that distract you from your main stream of thoughts.
3) Do you think that these things give you real pleasure or they are just a means of escapism?
4) Are you capable enough to handle these distractions that hinder you in achieving your goals?
5) Can you suggest some means to get rid of these hurdles which affect your aim of life?

Suggestive Activity

1) Make a list of all positive and negative traits that you have. Now think of ways how your positive traits can help you in overcoming the distraction in achieving your goals.

2) Prepare a list of all the negative traits that you would like to overcome and arrange those in the order "easy to difficult" to overcome. Choose the easy one first and get rid of the negativity.

Interesting Asides

Always remember that "The Best Success Stories Often Begin with Failure". Where there is a Will, there is a Way.

Goal setting is a must. You might think that the New Year's resolutions may or may not help. Research shows that people who set goals for themselves are more successful. In fact, according to goal management solution providers, people lose 30 per cent of their capacity and performance potential by not focusing on goals.

Arjuna's bird's eye test teaches you as to how you should set your priorities right and chase your goals. While others failed to separate their goal from distractions in their path, Arjuna was able to ignore everything else and keep his focus only on the prize. In life, there are so many irrelevant things that consume your energy on a day-to-day basis. You should always put the chaos aside and concentrate on the things that matter.

It is said that Edison failed in 360 attempts before he was able to successfully invent the electric bulb. His co-workers used to say that he was foolish because he had failed 360 times. Edison never paid any heed to his co-workers and used to consider that he was wiser in 360 ways, because by then, he knew what not to do to prepare the bulb.

Day to Day Relevance

Let your past not hinder your present. Forget the bitter experiences and move ahead in life with a better plan for your future. Facing your fears of failure will help you achieve your goal instead of running away from it.

Value Content

The strongest Mantra for success is "I CAN and I WILL". Believe you can do it. Believe you deserve it. Believe you will get it. Never let insecurity and negativity ruin your life. A positive attitude will lead to a positive outcome.

Questions to Assess

1) Who do you think is responsible for your low ranks?
2) What are the hurdles in your way to success?
3) List two ways about bringing change in your attitude?
4) What is the 4F formula?
5) How can you improve your self- esteem?
6) What is the best time to begin a good thing?

DAY 2
Intelligence

Dear Children,

Yesterday you were given the home task to do prayer before going to sleep and visualize that you are to add positivity in you. Tell honestly how many of you have really done this prayer. I know it is going to take time in gaining self-confidence, although it is in your hand. Sit in silence and pray to God. Pray to Him to pull you out safely from the clutches of the demon of negativity. Tell Him that you have been fighting all alone till now and that you have lost all hopes. Now imagine that you aren't alone any more. There is always someone who is there by your side, who is well aware of your condition and is competent enough to take you to the safer zone. Who is he?

You tell others that you have low vocabulary and you are unable to improve. Let me explain the actual vocabulary. Actual vocabulary is when a teacher teaches in a class and speaks out different words, you learn those words. So what is 'Actual vocabulary'? It means the information which a teacher expects from all the students of class which is given to all without any distinction and the same is to be reproduced by students. Some are able to recollect 100% and some can reproduce only a part of it. This partial reproduction is called 'Functional vocabulary'. So Actual vocabulary is the same for all but the Functional vocabulary differs and depends upon the level of seriousness one has put into the lesson. When there is any distraction, you can't be serious. More distraction means less Functional vocabulary.

Similarly your actual intelligence differs from your functional intelligence. But rest assured, actual intelligence is the same for all. Only thing is that you do not put your 100% and due to this, your functional intelligence reduces and people name it as low I.Q. Sometimes you may find that during your exams, you are not able to recall the concepts learnt earlier.

The reason for this difference is your lack of concentration or distraction. The more distraction, the less functional intelligence. From this, we may conclude that your functional Intelligence is not static. It varies individually and depends upon your state of mind, your interest in different subjects and your liking for a teacher.

Once your functional intelligence goes down, you start getting labelled by your teachers as Idiots, morons etc. But now you understand where the problem lies. You can't control all the factors that cause hindrance in your performance but it is in your hands to minimise the distractions resulting in an increase in your functional Intelligence. Let's think of the possible remedial measures to reduce your distractions which generally are:-
1) Lack of interest in studies
2) Not giving enough time for studies
3) Not being attentive during the class
4) Procrastination
5) Losing self-confidence
6) Not liking the teaching style of your teacher
7) No proper tuning with the teacher.
8) Wasting of time in non-productive matters.
9) Undesirable company.

There may be several reasons, best known only to you, about the distractions in you. What is going inside you? You are the maker of your own destiny. First and the foremost requirement is to know how to improve upon your academic performance. You must believe that there is no injustice done by GOD. The sun shines and gives equal light and warmth to all. It depends upon you how much you want and how you take it. You cannot blame GOD that someone is better placed. If someone is ahead of you, the reason may be that he/she probably has good guidance and support at home.

First of all, negativity has to be substituted by positivity. A feeling of inferiority always reduces your functional intelligence. The first step is to make up your mind and start. Starting is important because usually it takes little time to break the barrier. There are many examples from history to learn. You know Kalidas, who was considered the biggest fool on the earth. But because of being ridiculed by his wife once, he transformed and now his writings are a part of your curriculum. You hardly use 8-10 % of your brain. Rest of the brain goes to waste. First of all, prepare yourself mentally before starting the work. Face the challenge. There is no problem in the world without a solution but the solution is possible with effort only. You are no less intelligent than others but patience and perseverance are the two keys which are essential for the growth. You have to take a step first and rest lies in the hands of GOD. He wants every human being to excel. What is required is consistency of efforts for achieving success. Things which went wrong for years can't be rectified in days only. You can repair the loss by making good friends and by understanding the concept from the beginning. Merely cramming and memorizing is not going to help. Proper understanding of each concept of each subject is a must. In the beginning, it may take some time but one should not hesitate or be shy in asking the teacher to explain again. Tonight before you go to bed, make a written resolution and plan about how you are going to make efforts to achieve the target. Make your timetable and then don't compromise with it. Today might be your friend's birthday, tomorrow there could be a cricket match and next day, some guest might be coming. You have to set your goal and adjust yourself accordingly so that you achieve your goal. Your goal is that your functional intelligence and your actual intelligence should be the same. Remember, it is possible.

Assets :

Inquisitive Questions

1)   What do you mean by Intelligence?

2) Is it the same in all human beings? If it differs, what are the parameters to judge it?
3) What do you mean by the term I.Q.? Explain using some examples
4) Do we always face the challenges in our life wholeheartedly? Give reasons to support your answer?
5) Do you think that the challenges and obstacles help you succeed in the long run? How?
6) What is important to you — understanding the concept or just getting familiar with the concept at surface level as taught in the class?
7) How far do you agree with the statement --- "A little knowledge is a dangerous thing".

Suggestive Activity

1) Show some articles to the students and after showing these articles, ask them to write the names of the articles they had seen. If they are unable to reproduce the names, check about the reasons behind it. Check whether it is because of some distraction. Try to find that distraction.
2) Meditation and silent sitting and practising Yoga should be a part of curriculum so that the students could increase their concentration level and achieve success.

Interesting Asides

Einstein's memory was notoriously poor. He was unable to remember dates and could not remember even his own phone number. As a student, one of his teachers claimed that he had a memory like a sieve. But still he was awarded the 1921 Nobel Prize in Physics for his services to Theoretical Physics, and especially for his discovery of the law of the photoelectric effect.

Value Content

Winners embrace hard work. They love the discipline of it. The Losers, on the other hand, see it as a punishment. And that's the difference.

A dream doesn't become reality through magic; it takes sweat, determination and hard work. Without hard work, nothing grows but weeds.

Day to Day Relevance

It is generally observed that in almost all the educational institutions and schools, remedial classes are being held which is a way, turn active intelligence in the students to functional intelligence and improve their scores.

Questions to Access

1) What according to you may be the reasons for distractions in an ongoing class?
2) State the kinds of Intelligence.
3) What do you mean by Actual Vocabulary and Functional Vocabulary?
4) What kind of students are named as idiots, morons etc.?
5) Do you think God is to be held responsible that he has bestowed the intelligent students with extra wisdom? Is it His fault?
6) How can one achieve his aim? Write Do's and Don'ts for the same.
7) What are the practices required to attain growth?
8) When the sun rays are focused on a piece of paper, the paper starts burning. How is it possible? What inference will you like to draw from this phenomenon ?

Day 3
Magic Formula of 5D

You have now realized the impacts of the various distractions that reduce your functional vocabulary and must be thinking of ways to overcome them. I am sure by now, you must be feeling interested to work upon your academic weaknesses and attain your set goals. The Magic formula for this is 5 D. i.e.
1) Devotion
2) Discrimination
3) Discipline
4) Determination
5) Duty

Firstly, we'll talk about **DEVOTION**. Devotion means trueness, loyalty, dedication and adherence (towards some person or with some rules). In our context, devotion is to consider your teachers as supreme, listen to them very carefully and follow their instructions to the best possible extent (of your abilities). You cannot make a good beginning unless you have full faith in your parents and teachers. Your elders have gone through many phases of life and have experienced many such things you may not have. Whatever they want you to do, is for your benefit. Therefore, their ideas and advice must be accepted and followed with faith in them. As per Newton's third law of motion, every action has an equal and opposite reaction. The amount of your devotion towards your elders determines the quality of outcome. Just having faith in your teacher adds 10% to your performance. All you need to try is to live up to the expectations of your elders. Devotion is the foundation and if the foundation is strong, the structure will be strong.

DISCRIMINATION is the ability to find out the difference between what's wrong and what's right. During your life as a student, you will have to face a lot of challenges. All of you know the aim of your life or what you want to achieve in your life. There are two types of factors – first one that helps you in realizing your dreams and the other one that creates hurdles in your way to success by causing distraction or disturbance in your mind. You need to think of these hurdles and make a list of these on a piece of paper. You have come here to find a solution to your problems and to get the support (that you want) to proceed on the path leading to success. But the pressure of an undesirable company or other attractions may distract you from achieving your aim. You have to mend your mind, be determined and complete the game. Making correct choices at the right time would help you in writing your success stories in the years to come. Whereas making wrong choices during these precious years will ruin your entire life. You are to differentiate between the Right and the Wrong and to know when Wrong gets triggered.

DISCIPLINE is to follow a certain code of conduct or to obey certain rules. Once you start living a disciplined life, most of your negativity would automatically go away and things will gradually start falling into place. With discipline, you will be able to utilize your time in the most fruitful way. On the contrary, indiscipline wastes your most valuable resources i.e. time and energy that could have been fruitfully utilized for some meaningful purpose. Nature is the best example of discipline. Revolving of earth around the sun, rising and setting of the sun at a fixed time, movement of planets - everything in nature follows a system of discipline. Each entity of the universe, good or bad, has its own way to contribute to life or to nature. Discipline mainly depends on the control of senses. Once we control our senses, we would overcome a lot of self-generated problems in our life. Once the life is disciplined, you will be peaceful and will be able to take the right decisions.

DETERMINATION means firmness of purpose. Our senses play a very important role in our day to day life. It is difficult to control the temptations of these senses. A strong will power is required to gain control over the senses. This strong will power is known as determination. A systematic approach is required for this purpose. Once you are clear what you want to achieve and you are quite focused about it, it gets easier to gain control over your senses. You have to prepare yourself and become strong enough to avoid surrendering to inappropriate demands of the senses. Determination is the key factor that helps you to overcome the obstacles caused by these senses. If you add prayer to your determination, you would definitely overcome your weaknesses. Imagine the amount of happiness you are going to get when you overcome any of your bad habit.

Last but not the least is **DUTY**. You would be amongst the successful people, once you understand the duty assigned by God to you. Prepare a list of the assignments for yourself listing the kind of responsibilities you have as a student. What are your duties towards your school, teachers and parents? If you are taking care of the first four Ds and want to take up the assigned roles, it means that you are performing your duties. As a student your first and foremost duty is to go as per the law of society. You need to check and act accordingly as per the expectations the society has from you. Then only, you will be able to bring a desired change in yourself.

Assets :
Inquisitive Questions
1) Why is discipline so important in your life?
2) How do you distinguish between Love, Bhakti, Prayer and Devotion?
3) Differentiate between Prejudice, Bias and Discrimination.
4) How do you relate Courage to Determination?

Suggestive Activity
Just sit silently and write on a piece of paper about the kind of distractions you have in your life. Share your problems with your master. Ask for a solution. Check out for the number of problems that get solved by simply making you disciplined. Also, find out the

number and nature of problems that require determination for their resolution. Write down the conditions that trigger and compel you and distract you from the right goal.

Interesting Asides

The fourth Sikh Guru Ram Dass had many disciples who were always busy with their duties. Arjun Dev, one of the disciples, used to devote himself to the duty assigned to him. Guru Ram Dass had assigned the work of washing the utensils to Arjun Dev. Other disciples used to ask Arjun Dev as to why he was always busy washing the utensils? They also advised him to serve the Guru sometimes. Arjun Dev used to say that the work of washing the utensils was as per the Guru's orders. Other disciples claimed that only cleaning of the utensils was not the true service and that the Guru would not be pleased only with the cleaning of utensils. Arjun Dev always replied that he never tried to please the Guru and that his Duty was only to obey him.

When Guru Ram Dass' end was near, every disciple dreamt to be the successor of the Guru (because they thought that they had all the qualities of service and devotion in him). But the Guru had already finalized his 'will' for the announcement of his successor and declared that his 'will' should be opened after his death. When Guru Ram Dass left for his heavenly abode, everybody was eager to know the content of the 'will', but when the 'will' was opened, Arjun Dev had been declared the successor. Everyone was surprised and questioned why Arjun Dev was made the successor even though they had better qualities. The other disciples raised their voice and questioned the justification in making him the successor. Here lies the answer – Faith, Devotion and Discipline are the only prime qualities, not the knowledge and wisdom.

Day to Day Relevance

The 5Ds explained in this lesson should be the key mantras of one's life. We should discipline our children to save them from evils, to give them wisdom and to make them reflect upon God's wish. These 5Ds would help our children to grow, to become stronger, to be humble and learn the values of life.

Value Content

Devotion will lead to discrimination and discrimination to discipline and determination. Then duty will be a passion.

Devotion is the principal thing depicting your truth and dedication. I am devoted to none but truth.

Discrimination is the power with which we distinguish right from wrong.

Discipline is the strength with which we act rightly in the right manner at the right time and at the right place.

Determination is the power that guides us to act firmly and regularly.

I slept and dreamt that life was beauty,
I woke up and found that life was **Duty**.

Questions to Assess

1) How to develop the habit of discipline in yourself?
2) What is the secret of self-discipline?
3) You are talented, intelligent and ambitious, but you lack discipline and willpower. Do you think this can help you achieve your goals in life? Why? What can you do to improve?
4) There are 2 factors – passion and determination. Which would lead you to success out of these 2 factors?
5) Can one attain salvation by doing one's duties sincerely and being devoted to God?

4 Formulae (4F)

Formula for today is 4F i.e. Follow the master, Face the devil, Fight till end and Finish the game. By now you must have planned to **FOLLOW THE MASTER** and you know who the super master is. It is your super-consciousness that remained dormant in the beginning because you kept neglecting its voice. After cautioning you a number of times, the voice remained unheard. So now, it has become non-functional. Our previous discussions must have compelled you to feel the need for change. You must have made up your mind to bring a positive change in yourself. The most important is permission from your inner voice, i.e. your super conscious mind. If you want to make a correct beginning, prepare yourself mentally to follow the master. Master is a guru outside and a super conscious mind inside. Take benefit of their experience and start the process of eradicating the devil inside.

You should now take the 2nd step which is really an important one and it is **FACE THE DEVIL.** Yesterday, we discussed the role of 5Ds in our progress. One of the important ingredients of 5Ds is Determination. But it is not easy to get rid of old habits. From the word "HABIT", if you remove 'H', 'A bit' is left and even if 'A' is removed, 'Bit' is left. Now even if 'B' is removed, 'IT' is still left. It means to say that the old habits die hard. First and the foremost requirement is to get rid of a bad habit by proper planning, rationalisation and introspection. You should keep a personal diary. With a calm mind, first check the different types of devils present in you. You will have to be honest and firm with yourself. There should not be any excuse because you yourself are responsible for your present pitiable condition. In your diary, you should note down all your bad habits on priority (Devil 1, Devil 2……and so on). Give each habit a due space in your diary and introspect before bed time. Note down the number of times you give up to the temptations of bad habits. Start thinking about your own course of action on a daily basis. Prepare yourself well in advance to face the devil. Think about the course of action if the same situation arises next time. Keep a record for one month and gradually you would find that due to awareness, the frequency, intensity and duration of a wrong action/behaviour decreases. Chances of failures are there which may lead to frustration. Remember, failure is a step on the ladder to success. But you should not get disheartened.

On the contrary, a number of successful attempts may also lead to the development of ego. We should also not be overconfident about our success in a fight with the devils. Make it a regular practice to listen to your super-conscious (mind) and be quite firm that if a similar situation arises in future, you have already developed the confidence to a level that it would not create any more problems. Our thoughts are very powerful tools. Thoughts lead us to actions. Actions lead to habits. Our habits lead to character and character leads to destiny. Thus good thoughts lead to a good destiny and bad thoughts take us to a bad destiny. So we should develop a habit to keep a vigilant watch on our thoughts. Whenever a thought is generated in our mind, it should be approved by our heart i.e. the super conscious mind, before sending it to the hands (to make it practical). If the thought is good, we should try to implement it as fast as we can and if it is bad, we must try to eradicate it immediately (from the root). For example, if you get tempted to steal money from your own house, it is easier in the beginning to curb that temptation. But once you start stealing the money again, it would be difficult for you to restrict yourself in future and you start stealing money from your friends and others too.

It is always advisable to develop a habit of giving a thought before performing any task and ask your super conscious mind whether to do it or not. If it agrees with you, then you must go ahead but if it is indecisive, then you should strictly refrain yourself from doing that action. It can be understood better with an example of a lady who is alone in the house.

Before opening the door, she peeps through the pigeon eye of the door and if there is any suspicious person knocking at the door, she doesn't open the door and tells him to go back.

We should not give much time and space to negativity in our mind. Keeping a watch on our thoughts is very essential. We should be focused on the task that we are performing at present. If we are brushing our teeth, we should be completely focused on that task only. If we are eating food, our thoughts should be focused on chewing and eating only. This is the reason why specialists advise us not to eat food while watching TV because we swallow the unnecessary and waste thoughts (along with the food) that are generated by watching the TV.

3rd F is to **FIGHT TILL END**. This can be better understood with an example of a chain smoker. After realising the harmful effects of smoking on health, he makes up his mind to quit smoking. In the beginning, he resists its temptations for a few days. He also feels happy that he is shunting out a very bad habit from his life. But along with positivity in his mind, negativity also tries to deviate him from his determination. Your friends may pressurise you or your temptations may automatically get aggravated once again in their company. With Archimedes' principle, you will be able to understand this in a better way. According to this principle, there are two forces that act upon the body for it to float in the liquid. First one is the weight of the body and another one is the buoyant force of liquid. If the weight of the body exceeds, it sinks, but if the buoyant force is more than the weight of the body, it floats. Here your habit of smoking is your weight and your resolution to eradicate smoking is the buoyant force. If your resolution is strong, you will be able to quit this habit. But this principle is not always applicable in real life situations. It is dynamic in nature and depends on an individual or a situation. We can say *Savdhani hati to durghatna ghati.* To fight it till the end, you would have to practise continuously for at least 21 days and assess yourself thoroughly till you are sure that you have bid farewell to the temptation/habit and now nothing can put you back again on the old track. You must thank God for the same as it was because of His grace that you could fight till the end. Fighting till the end is necessary for two reasons. Firstly, if you are not able to eradicate any bad habit from the root, you will be a loser. Next time you will not gather enough willpower to start fighting again. Your self-confidence will be shattered and your morale will come down. Addiction will make you slave of your own thoughts and habits. Instead of becoming a master of your mind, you will become a slave of your senses.

What is **FINISHING THE GAME**? You have enormous problems inside you. With determination, you tried to solve a few of the problems and you succeeded. It is good that you could subtract one habit but, what about the remaining ones? Game is not yet over. It is just the beginning. Now your confidence level is high. Your success journey has made a remarkable beginning. Do not stop here, take up the next bad habit and start working on it. By taking them up one by one and with determination, you would be able to eradicate your bad habits and this is how this game would be over. Now your circumstances are favourable. If you stop here, you may not get this kind of situation next time. So, why wait? Once you are successful, you will feel more relaxed and peaceful. A day would come when you would be one of the most successful persons in this world. You will show the path to others by becoming a lighthouse. A day will come when you will be able to set an example for the generations to come. Vivekananda's advice to all of us is "Arise! Awake! And stop not till the goal is reached".

Assets :

Inquisitive Questions
1)	Have you ever been introspective to know your weaknesses?
2)	Do you know any person who has got rid of his bad habits?
3)	Have you ever imagined the kind of happiness you would feel, when you would get rid of the devil inside?

4) What is a good thought?
5) What is deep breathing?
6) It is said that we provide food to our body and mind through five senses. Is this correct? Explain your answer?

Interesting Asides

Gandhi Ji was a normal person with average performance
but he could finish the game of getting rid of the evils
within.

Suggestive Activity

1) Prepare a list of all your bad habits and fix your priorities to get rid of these habits. Decide, if you would go from difficult to easy or easy to difficult.
2) In case of a negative thought, go for deep breathing at least five times and observe its effects.

Day to Day Relevance

Many times you plan to get up early in the morning. You set
an alarm and also tell other members of the family to wake
you up. But you are also convinced that it is not possible to
get up early in the morning since you lack strong will power.

Value Content

We should never, never and never give up - Winston Churchil.

Question to Assess

1) What is better - to leave the bad habit at once or by reducing the frequency on a daily basis?
2) Facing the devil — is it physical or mental?
3) What will happen when we finish the game?

Day 5
The Mind

By now it must be clear to you that the mind is the root cause of all the problems and it is the mind that solves your problems. Mind is a good servant if you tame it but it is a bad master too. If you listen to the story of some prisoners, one common thing that can be concluded from their life experiences is that each one has committed the crime just because they could not resist the temptation of their mind at a particular moment. Now it depends on all of us, whether we make the mind our slave or a master.

To understand in detail, we will have to learn the concept of mind in depth. Mind is the outcome of thoughts generated by our five senses. To understand the concept better, we can classify the mind into 3 components-

1. Conscious mind
2. Subconscious mind
3. Super conscious mind

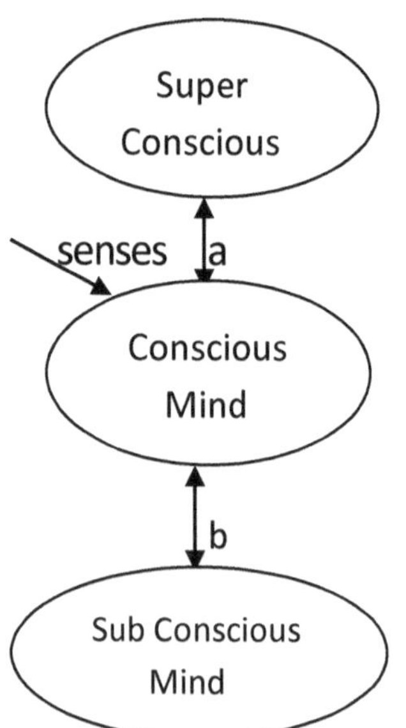

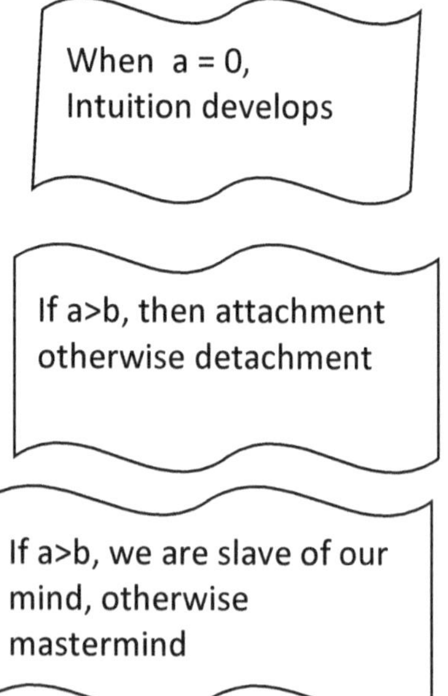

When we receive any message through our senses, the conscious mind becomes active. When you see something, the conscious mind captures the image and immediately sends the message to the subconscious mind which in turn stores that particular image. Our subconscious mind is already a store house of many such images, not of this birth but of many previous births too. When we receive any image through the conscious mind, the super conscious mind also analyses the quality of image, whether it is good or bad. Initially the voice of the super conscious mind is very clear but ignoring the call of the super conscious mind leads to feebleness of its voice. This is happening with all of you present in class. The reason for ignoring the warning of the super conscious mind is the intensity of your senses. Your liking or disliking for particular images differ from person to person. The food which is tasty for some may be disliked by others. The role of the subconscious mind cannot be ignored because of the choice or preferences in life for which our old impressions are responsible. We will understand it better with the following illustration - Suppose you pass through a fast food shop, you happen to see the eatables that are placed in the shop, your nose will like the smell and in spite of the call of your super conscious mind to avoid the food because of your ill health, you relish the fast food and ignore the warning of the super conscious mind. When these types of calls from the super conscious mind are repeatedly ignored by you, gradually you come under the grip of your subconscious mind that is already storing a lot of impressions of the present life as well as of the past births. Here the challenge is - how to make a decision for the right action, i.e. to make a correct choice between right and wrong. How to ignore a wrong action prompted by your senses?

The game here is interesting. If a person learns the art of listening to the super conscious mind and ignores the unjustified demand of senses and the subconscious mind, then one emerges a winner, otherwise a loser. Now, it is not always the case that the demand of the subconscious mind is unjustified. It depends upon the storage in the subconscious mind. This is the reason that sometimes in your class, you find a particular child is very good in one particular subject. The reason for this may be that his mind has retained some memory from his past birth. Whenever you try something new, the old memory of some similar experiences gets active. The memory of past birth that otherwise seems to get lost when we take birth, is not completely lost. A dim impression of the same is still there. Same thing is applicable for the negative traits too. If you were a chain smoker in your previous birth, the chances of getting addicted to smoking are more in the present birth. This is the reason that one must always make good choices and adopt healthy traits. It may be quite possible that you get the advantage of your previous births. Here the power of discrimination plays a very important role. It is always advisable to develop this power at an early age.

The efforts should be done so that your conscious mind is much closer to your super conscious mind and you may act as per the wishes of the super conscious mind. But when will it be possible? It will be possible only when the conscious mind is not so close to the subconscious mind because usually your subconscious mind compels you to go against the super conscious mind. A war between the two goes on throughout life and the winner is the one whom we listen more. The winner is the one who feeds the super conscious mind because the super conscious mind contains all the wisdom of the world. The person who goes as per the wishes of the super conscious mind, is never a loser. He becomes **good** first and later **great** too. The conscious mind must maintain a distance from the subconscious mind to reach closer to the super conscious mind. Another plan to get away from the negativity of the subconscious mind is to make it pure. The only way to make it pure, is to feed it with pure thoughts. Whatever impurities it contains, cannot be taken out. To raise the percentage of purity, the only solution is to add positivity and avoid adding more negativity. For generating positive thoughts, we should have the company of good books and good friends. We should read the autobiography of successful people. The ABC of life is to Avoid Bad

Company and _Always _Be _Careful. By keeping a watch on your thoughts and by not entertaining negativity from any of the senses, you can win the game of life. This reminds us of the three monkeys of Gandhi Ji, teaching us to See No Evil, Hear No Evil and Do No Evil. If we want to compensate for the loss that has already been done, the only solution is to raise the percentage of positivity of the subconscious mind and to get closer to our super conscious mind. When you get closer to the super conscious mind, you get power of intuition and our guess work starts getting more accurate. You become more focussed, more peaceful.

Assets :
Inquisitive Questions
1) What is the most complex organ in your body?
2) Which part of the body has the ability to make decisions?
3) Do you think that the decisions taken by your mind are always right?
4) How many of you still remember some bad and good moments of your childhood? Do you have any idea how you could remember them even now?
5) Have you ever heard of the subconscious mind?
6) Which part of the mind stops you from making wrong decisions?
7) Explain the meaning of "good and great" used in this lesson?
8) What is a pure mind?

Suggestive Activity
1) Teacher will put different kinds of objects like – erasers, toy cars , coloured pencils, markers of different colours, some colourful bands etc. in a box and will show it to the students twice. Afterwards the box will be covered with a cloth and students will be asked to write the name of objects. Your memory is sharp when your conscious mind is pure.
2) One session of meditation can be arranged for the students too.

Interesting Asides

1) **The subconscious mind records everything.** No matter if you're awake or asleep, the tape is running.
2) **The subconscious mind is always alert and awake.** When you fall asleep in front of the TV, your subconscious hears every single word that is being said.
3) The sub consciousness is one million times more powerful than the conscious mind. It speaks to you in dreams too.

Value Content

The super conscious mind is the soul, source, love and the authenticity in you. The subconscious mind is what you are. And the conscious mind is what you do, so always indulge into good practises.
*Just keep your conscious mind busy with expectations of the best.
*The subconscious mind is very powerful and with proper training, you can have a life where you are the "cause" rather than the "effect". Learn to be a driver and not the passenger.

Day to Day Relevance

1) It is said that the little children must be told value based stories in their formative period (till 7 years) and must be kept busy in some mind games—scribble /puzzles etc., because a child's critical mind only develops from around the age of eight. Therefore whatever they hear, see or feel, goes directly in the subconscious mind without analysis, and is accepted as fact. Since the subconscious mind never sleeps, the amount of data that goes directly in subconscious mind is phenomenal. You are literally everything in the eyes of your child. Whatever you tell them, their brain will record it as true.
2) If a person is bedridden for several years, he doesn't forget driving, his work or his routine as these get fixed in his subconscious mind and need not be taught again.
3) One can reach to the potential of Super Conscious mind by meditation, by spending quality of time in solitude and listening to

the voice of inner soul and heart which is also called 'surrendering to GOD'

Questions to Access

1) In how many parts can the mind be classified?
2) Which part of the mind stores all the images and can easily be termed as a storehouse?
3) Which part of the mind works as your well-wisher and warns you of making a wrong decision?
4) One must always make good choices and adopt healthy traits in his present life. Why?

DAY 6
Meditation

In the previous class, we had discussed the super conscious mind which provides us with the power of **intuition**. Let us discuss the meaning of the term 'Intuition' in detail. Intuition is the ability to understand something instinctively, without the need of conscious reasoning. Intuition is a special virtue which develops in a person and is related to a pure and calm mind. Power of intuition is very useful in a student's life too and helps him in many ways. Many times, a student gets confused while making choices or while discriminating between the right and the wrong. But surprisingly, our super-conscious mind knows the correct answer to all our questions. An ideal decision making is possible only if our subconscious mind is as active as our conscious mind. Our conscious mind is closer to our super-conscious mind in comparison to the subconscious mind. Problem of recall as well as retention is also solved when this kind of situation arises. Now we will discuss the techniques and the methods to purify our subconscious mind. We have already discussed a lot about these aspects. Before discussing any new step, let us first recap the related previous learnings.

1. To add positivity by learning good books and by keeping a good company.
2. By keeping watch on your thoughts. Only the thoughts that are approved by the super conscious mind must be turned into actions.
3. Each thought that is generated by our mind should pass the test of the heart.
4. See Good, Hear Good and Do Good.

Now let us discuss our further course of action. Is there any concrete strategy to bring the desired changes in yourself? The answer is 'Yes'. There are many ways to do so and the most powerful way is Meditation. The process of meditation is the same as we defrag computers to get faster output. Let me explain the process of defragmentation. When we copy any file to our computer hard disc, it is not necessary that we get contiguous space to store the file at one place. So the file gets stored (in a fragmented manner) at whatever and wherever the space is available. When we go for defragmentation, the computer creates the space in the hard disc and tries to adjust the file at such a place that whenever the need arises, it can be accessed easily. Similarly, meditation sets out our subconscious mind in order. It conditions our mind in such a way that it generates powerful and positive thoughts when the need arises and also helps to weaken the negative thoughts.

Further, I would like to tell you that different kinds of meditations have varied effects on our subconscious mind but ultimately the objective is to raise the quality of the subconscious mind and to set it in order to make it more positive. Before practising meditation, let us prepare a base for the same. This will prepare our mind for a peaceful experience. Chanting the word 'AUM' prepares one for meditation. This chanting is actually a healthy exercise for our windpipe. The first letter 'A' touches the lower part of our windpipe, 'U' the middle and 'M' the end. When we reach 'M', our lips get closed. Let us practise this exercise for a few minutes.

While reciting the 1st AUM, pray that you may see only what is good. Similarly :
- while reciting the 2nd AUM, pray that whatever you smell would be pleasant and pure.
- while reciting the 3rd AUM, pray that whatever you eat, would be satvik.
- while reciting the 4th AUM, pray that whatever you hear will be good for your ears and thoughts.
- while reciting the 5th AUM, pray that whatever you touch would be with pure intentions.
- while reciting the 6thAUM, pray that you only go to good places with your legs.

- while reciting the 7th and 8th AUM, pray that your body excretes properly, comfortably, regularly and completely and your body gets detoxified.
- while chanting the 9th AUM, pray that you carry out only the good work with your hands.
- while chanting the 10th AUM, pray that you speak politely and wisely and that you would think before you speak out the words.
- while chanting the 11th AUM, pray that you comfortably inhale good air, good thoughts and good habits.
- while chanting the 12th AUM, pray that you exhale impure air, bad habits and bad thoughts easily.
- while chanting the 13th AUM, pray that your digestive system works properly.
- while reciting the 14th AUM, pray that your blood flows through your body without any obstruction.
- while reciting the 15th AUM, pray that you have good thoughts only.
- while reciting the 16th AUM, pray that you grow physically well or your *annamaya kosha* should develop perfectly.
- While chanting the 17th AUM, pray that your *pran shakti* should be properly developed i.e. your body is ready to work actively with great enthusiasm. Your *pranyamaya kosha* would be fully developed.
- while reciting the 18th AUM, pray that your mental power is strong and you are mentally sound i.e. your *manomaya kosha* would be properly developed.
- while chanting the 19th AUM, pray that you are intellectually alert and your *vigyanmaya kosha* should be fully developed.
- while chanting the 20th AUM, pray that you are always blissful and your *anandmaya kosha* would be fully developed.
- while chanting the 21st AUM, pray that your mind becomes your slave.

This chanting of AUM for 21 times is illustrated in the following matrix:

1 See only what is good	**2** Smell only what is pleasant and pure.	**3** Eat only 'satvik' food
4 Hear only what is good for the ears	**5** Touch with pure intentions only	**6** Visit only good places
7 Let stool be passed regularly, completely and comfortably	**8** Let urine be passed regularly, completely and comfortably	**9** Carry out only the good work with the hands
10 Speak politely and wisely, think before speaking	**11** Comfortably inhale good air, good thoughts and good habits	**12** Exhale impure air, bad habits and bad thoughts
13 Digestive system works properly	**14** Blood flows through the body without any obstruction	**15** Create good thoughts using brain
16 Grow physically well (*annmaya kosha* to develop perfectly)	**17** Body works actively with great enthusiasm (*pranyamaya kosha* to develop perfectly)	**18** Mentally sound (*manomaya kosha* to develop perfectly)
19 Intellectually alert (*vigyanmaya kosha* to develop perfectly)	**20** Always be blissful (*anandamaya kosha* to develop perfectly)	**21** Mind should be your slave

This whole exercise is not going to take more than 5 minutes but these five minutes, if utilised properly before you begin your day's routine, would be beneficial for the whole day. Eventually, if any challenging situation comes in your life, this programming of your thought process would protect you. In our next class we would discuss some good meditational techniques.

Assets :

Inquisitive Questions

1) Do you carry the impression of your past births? What is the basis of your answer?
2) What is intuition?
3) How can you develop the virtue of intuition?
4) Do you think meditation is the process to be done only when you have retired? Why?
5) What do we mean by "thoughts approved by a super conscious mind"?

Interesting Asides

In a Sathya Sai school in Thailand, students devote 40% of their time to meditating and their results are far better than in any other school in Thailand.

If we divide the 35 minute period into three parts (5+25+5), the first 5 minutes and the last 5 minutes are for meditation.

Day to Day Relevance

Try to make your subconscious mind pure by visiting a temple, praying to GOD and make HIM your partner during the exams. Many times you will find the correct answer intuitively.

Value Content

You can see the bottom of a pond when the water is clean, stand still and there is no disturbance in it. In the same way, we can learn the process of seeing inside if we are calm and quiet. It is possible only through meditation.

Suggestive Activity

Draw the activity for each Aum in a serial order i.e.

1st : May my eyes see what is good only !

2nd : May my nose smell what is pleasant only !

3rd : May I always eat 'satvik' food !
and so on upto 21st Aum !

Questions to Assess

1) What is the benefit you are expecting from this exercise (Given under Suggested Activity)?
2) How much time is required to complete this exercise?
3) How meditation helps a student to become both good and great?
4) Can meditation help a student who is weak in studies? How?
5) Meditation is an essential part of the curriculum for the study of medicine, engineering and management. Why?
6) Tell the significance of 21 times, why not 25 times (HOT).

Day 7
More of Meditation

As discussed in the previous lesson, it is better if we do some physical exercises, even clapping just for two minutes and get the body ready for meditation. This exercise is going to be very effective. Keep clapping with full force for approximately two minutes till your palms turn red. This exercise will improve your retention level and will sharpen your memory. Once you start feeling positive changes in yourself, you can gradually increase the duration.

There are a number of meditational techniques, but today we'll discuss only the ones that are the best suitable for your age group. First of all, it is the choice of place for meditation. Always choose a silent zone with no outer sound. Concentrate your thoughts on breathing. Keep a close watch on inhaling and exhaling reflexes. You will see that time taken for inhaling and exhaling will keep reducing continuously. A stage will come when the time taken for inhaling and exhaling will feel like almost zero. Don't put conscious efforts to reach at this stage. It is a natural process and to attain this level, you should have the patience, perseverance and regular practice. It may take a great deal of practice. It is recommended that you should practise it at the same place and at the same time, in the beginning. Once this stage is reached, you will feel lighted. Cosmic energy, which is present in the atmosphere, will start entering you. This energy will act on those areas where your energy flow is minimum. You can term these areas as 'The areas of red patch'. Gradually you will start feeling that your energy level is rising. Your desire to work hard will also rise. But it will depend on the amount of time that you would invest in practising this drill. The more the amount of time and practice spent on this activity, the more will be your realization that your anxiety and anger levels have reduced. It will give a boost to your retention levels and memory. Your urge and desire to learn will increase and your laziness and procrastination tendencies will reduce. The positive results of meditation prove that it is truly worth investing time in it.

The 2nd type of meditation is the light meditation. It is very effective. It gives better results if practised early in the morning. Light a lamp or candle and take care that the flame is not flickering. If it flickers, it is better to put a flame guard around it. Place the flame at the level of eyes, by adjusting its height. Sit comfortably with a straight back. Insulate yourself from the ground by sitting on something made of wood or wool. Remember to say a prayer to God. Seek HIS help for the right and effective meditation. Take several deep breaths and practise *'Anulom Vilom'*. Take care of your breath. While inhaling say "SO" and while exhaling, say 'Hum'. Recite AUM 21 times. We have already discussed AUM and its chanting process in the previous lesson.

Now gaze at the flame of the candle, which is placed at eye level. After a few seconds of fixing your gaze on the light of the candle, close your eyes. You would be able to see a reflected image of flame. If you are not able to see it, open your eyes and continue to focus on the flame again. Diffuse this light through inside your head. Make sure that it touches every cell of your brain. Feel that your intellect is being illuminated through this light. Slowly and gently draw the flame into the region of your spiritual heart and visualize it in the petal of a lotus flower. You can keep the image of your deity at the centre of light. Imagine as if the petals of the lotus are being opened one by one, illuminating your heart. Wash every thought, every feeling and each emotion in that light, dissolving all shadows. There is no corner where darkness can hide. The light spreads even more brightly and becomes even more intense. With the effect of light, the negative feelings vanish. Now contemplate – "I feel that love embraces all things....I am Truth..... I am Purity....... I am Peace...... I am Love....... Non-violence...... Compassionate....... Happy and a tolerant soul". Give a pause of a few seconds between each quality.

Now allow the light to enter every part of your body. Visualise that the light reaches your limbs, feet, toes and fingers. Then generate good thoughts, "My feet carry me to only good places, where GOD wants me to go".

Then the light rises to the left shoulder, the arm and the hand and then to the right side. Then visualise - "My hand will do only the good work". Let the light rise to the throat and the head and talk to yourself - "I will speak only the truth and whatever my super conscious mind guides me". Visualise that the light reaches your eyes and ears and then tell yourself, - "I will see good only and I will hear good only". Then visualise that the light reaches your mouth and tell yourself, - "I will speak pleasing truth and I will eat only righteous food. Now visualise that the light enters your nose and tell yourself, - "I will smell only what is good for me". Continue to visualise that the light has entered your head and then tell yourself, - "My head has become pure and carries good thoughts only". Soon the light would occupy all the available space of your body.

Imagine that I am an epitome of light and the light is becoming more intense. It is spreading and diffusing in all directions. The light that is present inside as well as the light outside, is the only reality. The membrane of the body no longer separates me from anything else. The body too is all light. Now start visualising, - "I am not merely a soul, but an image and likeness of God. This light includes everything and everyone. I am the one with all the persons whom I love - relatives, friends and companions. I am also the one with all those who are not friendly with me, or who want to harm me or even govern me. I am the one with all the entities of the universe i.e. animals, vegetables, grass, forests etc. I am the one with minerals, rocks, mountains, lakes, seas, planets, solar system, galaxy, cosmos and more. My light is the light of the entire universe". Visualise the form of God (whichever form you worship). Visualise the oneness with God. Say a prayer.

"Lord, my strength, my defence, my refuge, my liberation, O God, my king, be with me always". Then do the breathing exercise. Bring the light back to your heart that will guard you through the day and night. Now rest for a while, lie down, if possible, take some rest. Now slowly open your eyes.

Assets :

Inquisitive Questions

1) Do you feel that you are silent when you are told to sit quietly in the classroom?
2) What happens in your mind when you are sitting silently?
3) Do you sometimes feel stressful, angry, and revengeful?
4) What do you do to overcome such feelings?

Interesting Asides

- Archimedes discovered the law of buoyancy while taking a bath and ran through the streets to announce his discovery.
- The young Isaac Newton was sitting in his garden when an apple fell on his head and he suddenly came up with his theory of gravity.
- Unless we tune in the transistor at the proper wavelength and frequency, we would not be able to listen to anything.
- There is an amusing story about Alexander the Great. When he came to India, he found that the Indians were a race of brave and fearless people. He made friends with them. When he was about to return to his country, he remembered that his people had asked him to bring to them an Indian yogi. They had heard a lot about yogis and were very desirous of seeing one, meeting him, hearing him speak and receiving his blessings. Alexander was told that the yogis dwelt in the forest. In quest of a yogi, he went to a forest. He found one sitting underneath a tree in deep meditation. He waited patiently until the yogi opened his eyes, shining with a strange and mystic light. Reverently, Alexander requested the yogi to accompany him to

Greece, saying. "I will give you everything you need or ask for. But, please come with me. My people would love to meet you!" The yogi quietly answered, - "I need nothing, I am happy with what I have and where I am!" This was the first time that anyone had turned down Alexander's request. He could not control himself. He flew into a rage and unsheathing his sword, he thundered, "Do you know who is speaking to you? I am the great king Alexander. If you do not listen to me, I will kill you and cut you into pieces!" Unperturbed, the yogi answered - "You cannot kill me! You can only kill my body. And the body is nothing but a garment I have worn. I am not the body. I am that which dwells within the body! I am not the "deh". I am the "dehin"- the dwelling one!" The yogi continued, - "You say that you are a king. May I tell you who you are? You are my slave!" Stunned, Alexander asked. "How am I a slave of your slave?" In a voice tender with compassion, the yogi explained. "**I have mastered anger.** Anger is my slave. See, how easily you gave way to anger. You are a slave of anger, and, therefore, a slave of my slave!".

Day to Day Relevance

Regular meditation reduces hyperactivity and helps in anger management. It improves health by decreasing stress, pulse rate etc. It improves memory and retention power.

Suggestive Activity

- Take a convex lens and focus the sunlight on a piece of paper. This concentrated light will burn the paper.
- Put some water in a large trough then put various coloured stones and some vegetation at the bottom. Now disturb the top layer of water so that a lot of ripples are created in water. Try to see the things lying at the bottom of the trough. Now wait for some time. Let water become stable and calm. Now you will be able to see the things lying at the bottom.

Value Content

1) Meditation will interrupt the cycle of negative thoughts like resentment, dissatisfaction and desire for revenge. It will bring inner stillness and give your mind a new direction.
2) It will increase values like patience, calmness, creativity, self-confidence and positivity.

Questions to Access

1) How many meditational techniques are discussed in this lesson?
2) How will meditation help in character building?
3) How is meditation helpful for a student?
4) Write a dialogue with God.
5) Prepare a guided meditation tour from a topic of a subject which you find difficult.
6) What are the benefits of developing intuition?
7) Practice any one technique for 10 minutes every day and note down results after 1 month.
8) What is your opinion – whether Meditation is an activity for the teen or for the old age person?

Day 8
Anger Management

It is a common scene everywhere to notice incidents of destruction due to anger. We no longer have any patience and the anger inside us is ready to ignite with a little spark. This can be seen anywhere. You would have noticed people on a road blowing the horn repeatedly without knowing the situation of the car in front of them. Children are no longer an exception. You can occasionally see various arguments ending with hand to hand fights in front of the schools. Reason is ANGER, a word short by one alphabet from DANGER. Frankly speaking, anger is the prime cause of unhappy families, broken houses, divorced couples and many more. People are observed breaking their TV sets after being defeated by a rival country in a cricket game. Till they realize their mistake, it is too late. The loss caused due to the anger is, most of the time, irreparable. The first attack of anger is on the power of discrimination between the right and the wrong. Person loses his sense and most of the criminal activities take place because of anger only. Anger is the prime reason for over 70% of prisoners in jail. After the seizure of anger, you feel as if your whole body is shaking like the land after the tsunami. Generally it takes too much time to reset yourself. Even suicide is one of the gifts of anger itself. Psychologists advise not to take food immediately after the rage of anger because the energy that evolves from food at that time, is also negative. It is one of the six vices present in every human being. Although most of us possess anger, its quantity varies from person to person. It is one of the major problems of adolescents and is responsible for the present condition of our world, where war, distrust, enmity is prevailing. Anger is a loaded weapon, be careful where you point it. You are not sure when it will attack. In a nutshell, anger has long lasting effects on your body, mind and spirit.

To start with the origin of anger, we will have to go to Darwin theory, which states that man is a product of animals. When we become humans, still some of the animalism is left inside us. Different animals possess different kinds of animalism. The person with a lot of in-built anger may be the product of cat, tiger or such animals having quality of anger. Anger is directly linked with our desires, which are prompted because of our senses. If a desire is fulfilled, it gives birth to advanced desire and if not, it gives birth to the anger. Sometimes we hold grudges against the person who has done some kind of injustice to you and instead of forgiving and forgetting his mistakes, we wait for the appropriate time to strike him to satisfy our ego. Now several questions arise :-

- Should we continue like this or start thinking about managing the anger?
- Are we thinking that it is beyond our capacity or potential to control it?
- What will happen if I continue with anger?
- Is my anger helping me anyways or anywhere?
- Am I gaining any advantage because of this situation?
- Is there any way out?

Three more questions that you need to answer are :-
1. Is it important to manage the anger?
2. Is it possible to control it?
3. Can I control it?

If the answer of these three questions is 'Yes', then we have to start working upon it and ask ourselves about three new questions related to anger :-
1. What is the intensity?
2. What is the duration?
3. What is the frequency?

Now, where to start from? Analyse your priorities. Your desire to get rid of the anger will be strong, once you ponder over the harmful effects of anger. Let us think and analyse the effects of anger on physical, mental and social domains.

You may get angry because of three categories of people. First who is at a higher platform than you, may be your parents or elder sister or elder brother or teachers. Second who is at an equal status like your friends. Third, who is at a lower place like your juniors in school or your younger brother or younger sister. When you get angry at elders, it creates mental agony in you. Of course now-a-days mothers are like friends so you don't consider them at a higher platform, but what about the teachers? They are not going to tolerate your nuisance. Instead, when you lose your impression in them, you get deprived of many privileges too. Physical impact of the same is that you lose your appetite. You lose the company of good friends who will avoid displaying any sort of friendship with you to the teachers. Glossy look on your face goes missing. It is going to single you out in your class and this is going to affect you mentally. Chances of frustration cannot be ruled out. There are chances of emotional deadlock between you and the elders which you cannot afford for your future growth. It is going to affect your stamina, retention power and ability to cope with the adverse situations, which are bound to come since these are part and parcel of life. When the frequency of you getting angry increases amongst your friends, you start losing your friends. You are tagged as HWC (Handle With Care). Chances of your social boycott cannot be ruled out. You no longer would be getting attention and/or sympathy from your peer group. When you get angry towards your youngsters, they feel helpless. Sometimes they take the help of someone stronger and you may get into some trouble. All such circumstances are hindrance in your physical, mental and social growth. You will agree that anger does not serve any purpose and it only makes you unpopular in your own social circle. You will lose your peace of mind which is pretty expensive as compared to all your other possessions. If you do not take any action now, you may be the victim of chronic diseases like high BP, diabetes, cardiac problems etc. in future. Many cases of brain stroke and paralysis are the outcome of anger only.

By now you must be convinced that it is urgent as well as important to get rid of the anger. Some of you may be thinking that this has been inherited from your father and that there is no solution to it. You will have to pass your life with such angry nature only. But you are wrong here. Again I must remind you of the magical formula of 4F, suggested by Sri Sathya Sai Baba - it is, Follow the master, Face the devil, Fight till end and Finish the game. When you are aware of the devil, there is no other alternative except to listen to your master. Master can be a book of experiences of those who could manage their anger. Instead of doing your own research, it is better to take guidance from the experience of others. The most important is self-analysis. Just sit silently and ask yourself what is more disturbing when you are angry - is it intensity or the frequency or duration? Then visualize the past experience of anger, just check for the perimeters that triggered your anger. Here one thing I would like to emphasize that you cannot hold anyone else responsible for your anger. You must admit that you are yourself responsible for your anger. No one else can make you angry till you desire. I know this statement is going to disturb you, but it is a fact that without your consent, no one else can make you angry. Once you digest this statement, we can move further.

"The wars are fought in the mind and not outside" says Napoleon. It means that the thoughts are responsible for every war. So when you start thinking in shoes of the other person, you have a regard for his nature, you understand that whatever he has done, is because of his nature and you won't be angry with him. Rather, sometimes you will have empathy for him. Remember, it is very difficult to change any one. It is even difficult to change yourself but it is possible. Again you need to follow the 5D's - these are Devotion (firm faith in yourself and your master), Discrimination (between right and wrong), Discipline, Determination (to change yourself) and your Duty. With these 5Ds, it is possible to reduce it to a great extent, though may not be fully.

Whenever you are angry, it will be difficult for you to lie down. Anger is going to flourish once you get up. So if you want to get rid of anger, then lie down and take rest – physically and mentally. Take deep breaths, divert your thoughts to something constructive, leave the place of incidence and move somewhere else. Even recitation of Gayatri Mantra will make you cool. See your face in the mirror and you won't like your own face. Face with a smile is attractive, but not an angry face. You will not like to see your ugly and angry face. Drink two glasses of water. Take deep breaths and start observing your breath, you will feel relieved. Once you are able to let go off some time, you will be able to manage the anger. It is well said that "**Speak when you are angry and you will make the best speech you will ever regret**." Although it is difficult, but if you control your tongue, you will reduce the intensity and the duration of anger. Remember "**The greatest remedy for anger is delay**." Once you decide not to do anything in your present state of anger, you will save yourself from the ill-effects of anger. You can program yourself in such a way that before giving any reply, you will make a pause and then only speak out. With this practice, you will be saving yourself from anger, even in the normal situations. Once you are aware of your problems, then half of the job is already done. Again my advice to you is - if you get angry any time, then regretting is all right but don't get frustrated. Cursing yourself is sign of inferiority complex, instead do your own self-analysis and plan for avoiding anger in future. Once you get determined, you will automatically get the wisdom of getting rid of problems. Still if someone gets pleasure in making you angry, consider that GOD, in the form of that person, is taking your test to check, how much you have improved. Initially, it may be difficult, but I am sure that you will be able to pass the test with distinction in the end. Just visualize how happy you will be after finishing the game in flying mode. You will be able to enjoy the frustration of the person who was trying to make you angry. The real defeat is when your inner conscience accepts the defeat. Let us avoid that situation. Ask GOD to help you to get rid of this devil inside you. This is the right time to strike because you are in a position to change your habit now. Once you cross your teen age, it will become chronic. Just tell yourself that "I am a human being and not a dog. I will not hand over my remote in the hands of others". No one, except you, can change yourself. After some time, this change will be visible to all and people will compliment you. Just visualize the glow on your face even now. This visualization will help you and serve as a motivation for your future. Sometimes you may feel that without getting angry, your parents and your friends don't take your work seriously and you have no alternative but to get angry, but this formula does not work longer. Very soon, they will get accustomed to your anger. This process is not going to affect anyone for a longer period. What will be your fate then? Imagine if you have to burn someone else's hand with a hot charcoal and you place the charcoal with your hand on the hand of another person, will it be possible to save your own hand?

It is written in the holy Quran that the pledge taken during the rage of anger can be terminated and this will not be considered as Sin. Probably the justification of the fatwa is that the person during the rage of anger does no longer remain the original one and his intellectual capacity is no longer valid. We are to act and not to react. Sometimes anger is required too. Can a soldier fight with enemy without anger? Sometimes it is necessary to get angry, but it should not be taken as an excuse. If you are seeing that injustice is being done to a weak or helpless person and you keep silent, it will also be a sin. This world is not suffering because of violence of unjust persons, it is suffering because of the silence of good persons. If you remain silent to the injustice and do not use your anger on wicked persons, you will repent later on your own act. Of course, we have to manage the anger and it is to be used as and when required for the right purpose and at the right time. Try to act from the upper surface without burning your own heart. Remember that it is the game of thoughts. Once you start this game, have the remote in your own hand and become master of your own mind. The moment you know, when and how to get rid of the angry thoughts, you will be the **_MUQADDAR KA SIKANDAR_**.

Assets :

Inquisitive Questions

1) Do you have trouble controlling your own anger?
2) Do you worry about how angry you sometimes feel?
3) Have you ever ended a relationship or friendship with someone because of how they behaved when they were angry?
4) Have you ever noticed the ill effects of Anger?

Interesting aside

If you are angry with your juniors, count 1 to 10 before taking any action. If you are angry with your equals, count from 1 to 30. If you are angry with your seniors, count from 1 to 100, but if you are angry with your teacher, better keep counting.

Suggested Activity

Role play: Teacher will ask two students to volunteer. One of them is to provoke the other and make him angry. The role of the second student is not to get angry. Teachers can repeat this activity by taking selected children. The one out of the two who is not to get angry, should be the child who usually gets angry. There are two possibilities:

Case – 1 : The child who usually gets angry, will not get angry in spite of the provocation by the other child. We will be able to prove that once we know that the person in front of you is testing you, we will win over.

Case – 2 : When the second child gets more angry, note down the time taken to get angry. Repeat discussing the cause of anger with him.

Day to Day Relevance

Usually, the victim of anger is a student, because of his immaturity, innocence and inexperience. The following casualties result into anger:

1. Listening and reasoning ability
2. Memory loss i.e. receiving, retaining and recalling abilities
3. Problem solving ability
4. Ability to make the right decision.

Wastage of time and energy are the by-products. Angry nature makes him/her impatient and intolerant. All such negative traits are not conducive to his/her desire to excel in studies and life.

Value Content

We should **act** and not **react** to someone who criticizes you.

Questions to Assess

1) How do people express their anger over phone, computer, TV and office files?
2) How do people express themselves in a road rage?
3) How is jealousy related to increased anger?
4) Is there any relation between desire and anger?
5) "The person who has ample stock of love cannot get angry". Support your answer (HOT).

Day 9
Power of Prayer

By now, you know the ways to acquire peace and the importance of having a peaceful and relaxed mind. It was because of his peaceful nature that Arjuna won the battle of Mahabharta, but on the contrary, it was the lack of peace due to which Karna lost the same battle. After doing any wrong deed, hurting someone or committing any crime deliberately or non-deliberately, your peace of mind gets robbed. You begin to have sleepless nights. The actions once performed, can't be undone. It's like an irreversible chemical reaction, the changes that occur once, cannot be revived. The only solution is repentance and prayers. By offering prayers, you can regain your peace of mind. Prayers have immense healing power and praying is a highly useful activity in our day to day life and living. I would like to share with you some of the real life stories that I have personally experienced.

Illustration 1: Our school building was under construction and a lantern for the roof was planned. It was a major milestone in the history of the institute. Approximately 300 bags of cement were placed under the open sky. All of a sudden, the sky was unexpectedly covered with dark clouds and it was apparently about to pour in no time. The entire atmosphere was filled with anxiety because it was not possible to stack the cement bags inside in such a short time. An unprecedented loss was foreseen that could have further created more trouble as all other preparations were going to be hampered. An emergency meeting was called and each staff member was instructed to go to their respective classes and advise the children to pray collectively. All of sudden, black clouds started scattering and surprisingly, we managed to construct the slab. Just after the desired amount of work was completed, it started raining cats and dogs. It was indeed the power of prayers of the children that saved us from heavy losses.

Illustration 2: Another personal experience would highlight the importance of a prayer. It is a real episode in the life of one of our drivers, who accidently got burns on his leg. It got so severe that he was unable to bear the pain and was to be admitted in a local private hospital. When I visited him to inquire about his condition, he complained of the pain that he had to undergo at the time of dressing. During those days, I used to teach Maths to students of 10th class. The next day, I asked my class to pray for the driver and asked God to help him with a painless dressing of his wounds. We earnestly prayed for the same. Next evening, when I visited him again and enquired about his condition, he told me that the dressing was not at all painful. Thereafter, praying for him became a daily routine of my class. Every evening, I used to ask him about his dressing experience and he used to tell me that dressing had become painless. Due to some reasons, one day we could not pray for him in the class. On the same day, I got to know that the driver experienced acute pain while dressing his wounds.

Illustration 3: Once I was watching a cricket match with my nephew on the TV. The match was being played between India and Pakistan and India was losing the match. All of a sudden, I asked my nephew to pray if he wanted India to win. He instantly started reciting *Gayatri Mantra*. I too started praying to GOD to help as I wanted that the young boy should develop a faith in the power of prayers. My concern was not the cricket match, but it was my nephew. I prayed intensely. All of a sudden, the scenario changed and the Indian team started winning the match. Many of you may think that it was a chance victory and the credit should not be given to the prayers. But dear children, it is not the only time that I have experienced the power of prayers.

I do not say that you can take this chance every time and that you will get what you want, without putting in your own efforts. But prayers always play a very important role in our lives. You must try and experience it yourself and I am sure that you will also endorse my view.

In addition, the quality of the prayer also matters. A prayer with doubt in mind, with ego in heart or without intensity will not serve the purpose. If you want the water to flow from one vessel to the other without any external pressure, then there should be a difference of levels in the water vessels. The source vessel should be positioned at a higher platform than the receiving vessel. Our ego should weigh less. There should not be any blockage in the pipe that facilitates the flow of water. That blockage in the water pipe symbolizes doubts. The end of the pipe should be positioned deep enough in the source vessel from where the water is to be flown. It symbolizes that the intensity of prayer should be quite high. If you feel that your prayer is not being answered, then you need to accept the fact that whatever you are seeking is not favourable to you or your heart lacks the amount of faith that is required for the prayers to be fulfilled.

Nowadays, there are many kinds of stresses that you might be carrying in your heart. Unfortunately, there might be some kind of problems that you can't share with anyone. In such a case, prayers can sooth you and provide relief to your aching heart. When you feel that there is no one by your side and no one understands your view point, consider God as your best friend and share your problem with Him. But you should love God and should not consider God as someone who punishes you. The pain and miseries in your life are the results of your own karmas for which you will have to face the consequences in the form of suffering. But if you take shelter under God's umbrella, then God can reduce the sufferings to some extent. This is similar to a person getting some relief from the scorching heat of sun or from rain using an umbrella. You feel thankful to your friends who bring you gifts. Similarly, you must be thankful to God for this life and his abundance of blessings in different forms. It is part of your duty to offer gratitude to Him.

Assets :

Inquisitive Questions

1) Do you believe in the Power of Prayer? Why? Give an example in support of your answer.

2) Have you ever been witness to the power of Prayer? Describe the outcome.

3) Do you feel that true prayers can be done only in the temples or other places of worship or can the prayers be done anywhere? Why do you feel so?

4) If you pray that your friend should live longer, would this prayer make him/her live longer?

Interesting Asides

Once, there were three friends in a park and were discussing the best positions for doing a prayer. An electricity repairman was also working nearby to repair the broken cables. One of the friends claimed : "Kneeling is the best position to pray". The second friend denied and claimed : "When I stand with my hands outstretched to the sky, I get the best results." The third friend said that both of them were wrong and insisted : "The most effective prayer position is lying face down on the floor."

The electricity repairman was tired and could not tolerate their claims. He shouted "Look at me, the best prayer I have ever done was when I was hanging upside down from an electricity pole".

Suggestive Activity

There is a five finger prayer game. Younger children will learn best prayers and remember the concepts. To carry out this five finger prayer game, assemble the class children and ask them to hold their hands together in a prayer position. Each finger tells us the concepts of the prayer and reminds us what to do :

- the thumb is positioned closest to us

- the index/pointer finger tells us the direction
- the middle finger stands above all others
- the ring finger is weaker than others
- the pinky (little) finger is the smallest.

a) Look at your **Thumb** and Say a prayer for those **closest to you (your parents or your siblings)**.

b) Look at your **Pointer Finger** and Say a prayer for your **school teachers** who guide you at every step.

c) Look at your **Middle Finger** and Say a prayer for the **Head of the country.**

d) Look at your **Ring Finger** and Say a prayer for a **sick person** or **someone in a serious need.**

e) Look at your **Pinky (little) Finger** and Say a prayer for **yourself.**

Day to Day Relevance

1) A prayer is the most important activity we can do to get closer to GOD. It can bring light to darkness, change our mind set, protect us and our loved ones, bring breakthroughs in our life, overcome distressing circumstances, avoid misfortunes and always bring positivity.

2) Prayer should not be to harm others directly or indirectly.

Value Content

Prayer is all positive. Every word uttered during a prayer with a pure heart and pure mind releases us from fear, pain, agony and miseries. Prayers are equally necessary for our existence.

Questions to Assess

1) What do you think are the prerequisites for effectiveness of the prayer?

2) Do you think that the fortune of a person can be changed with the prayers?

3) When I pray, I end with the words "in Bhagwan Sathya Sai name" and all my mental trauma vanishes and becomes zero. Have you ever felt something like this?

4) Do you think that "mantras" also work like prayers?

5) What would someone hope to gain when they want to pray to a) Lakshmi, b) Saraswati, c) Sathya Sai ?

6) How do prayers help a brilliant as well as a weak student especially in studies?

7) Create a best prayer for the night that you would like to share with GOD. (HOT).

Day 10
Gayatri Mantra

Today we will discuss more about prayer. We'll discuss the ideal time to pray and which type of prayer is considered the best. Different prayers mainly serve different purposes. But as already discussed, a prayer with the right intention and intensity helps us to establish a strong connection with God. Some prayers are to be offered when you wake up. Some are to be offered at the meal time and there are some prayers that are to be offered during the bed time. We should make sure that we must pray with a humble heart. The prayer that is best suited for the students is the *Gayatri Mantra*. Now let us discuss the meaning and importance of Gayatri Mantra. There is a famous mythological story. This mantra had been discovered by Rishi Vishwamitra. Once Rishi Vishwamitra was performing a yajna and king Indra sent a nymph named Menaka to distract him from the yajna. Somehow, Menaka succeeded in distracting him from the Yajna. This compelled Vishvamitra to think that - if the negativity could distract him besides being such a legendary sage, then what would be the plight of a common man who is not much competent to bear the negativity? Therefore, he composed a mantra for the welfare of the masses, so that this one mantra should act as a buoyant force for a common man who is suppressed under the weight of negativity. The most important element required for a prayer to be fulfilled is to have faith in its magical effects. Importance of this fruitful Mantra is very well accepted by all. By reciting Gayatri Mantra, you can get rid of three kinds of deficiencies in your life. These are —

    a)   Deficiency of knowledge
    b)   Deficiency of power
    c)   Deficiency of basic needs

All of us want to be free from the above three deficiencies in our life.

There are two stages in a man' life –

1. **Full life stage** is the one in which a person is ready to do any purposeful work or to face any challenge (that comes his way), successfully.

2. **Half life stage** – Any person who is going through this stage, usually works only if there is some sort of compulsion or some external stress. He/She does not enjoy doing any work. As a student, you are supposed to do the homework given by your teachers. You do the homework, just because of fear of punishment or to be in the good books of your teachers. Sometimes you simply work from head to hand without taking heart into consideration. Sitting in front of a T.V, you tend to copy from unaccepted sources (like the internet or so), just for the sake of completing your homework due to fear of the teacher. These all are the characteristics of a person going through a half life stage. During this phase of life, we feel that there is no hope left and we can't bring any positive change in ourselves. The role of Gayatri Mantra is to shift a person from half life stage to full life stage. At present, you may not be very convinced with the impact of this mantra and you may feel that it is beyond your comprehension. But when you practice continuously, you will realise the power of this Mantra that establishes a strong connection with Almighty God and brings positive changes in your life. Just think for yourself and realize at which stage of life you are?

Gayatri Mantra can be divided into 5 parts –
The 1st part of mantra is *AUM* and you already know that Aum is the first name of GOD. Even NASA has recorded the sound of the rays coming from the sun and that sound is AUM. This sound can travel even through the vacuum. This sound is omnipresent.

The 2nd part of the mantra is *Bhur bhuva swah*. These three words represent all the qualities of GOD which is triplicate in nature i.e.
- the one who creates, organises and destroys

- who is the most knowledgeable and knows about past, present and future
- who is the owner of Paatal Lok, Prithvi Lok and Aakash Lok.

3rd part of the mantra is *tat savitur vareniyam*. Here *tat savitur* is pointing towards the Sun, one of the trailers of GOD. If you want to know the quality of God, then look at the Sun that is completely impartial, that only gives energy, heat and the comforts of life and that doesn't ask for anything in return. *Vareniyam* means someone whose attributes are worth adoption.

The 4th part of the mantra is *Bhargo, devasihe, dhimahi*. Here, *Bhargo* means someone who can destroy the negativity, *Devasiye* means the one who only gives and *Dhimaye* means the one whom I meditate upon. So till the 4th part, we have praised God and have meditated.

The 5th part is *dhiyo yo na pracho dayat,* which means that we pray to God to grant wisdom to everyone. The mantra is actually three in one. We begin with praising God, then we meditate upon and then ask for the boon and the boon looks selfless in nature. We don't ask wisdom for any particular individual, rather we pray for the entire human race. So, if we combine all the 5 parts, the meaning of the mantra is the God Himself –
- whose first name is Aum
- who has many attributes of triplicate nature
- whose one trailer is Sun
- whose act is worth adoption
- who destroys the existing evils and who only gives (does not take anything)
I meditate to God and ask for a boon that HE must give us all wisdom of good quality.

My dear students, you need not take out any special time from your studies for the mantra. While carrying out your daily chores, you can keep chanting this mantra in your heart anytime. The best time considered to recite this mantra is early morning or during sun set in the evening. But otherwise every time is the best time for it. Recitation of mantra will save you from all the evils of life. Empty mind is the devil's workshop. It's better to utilize the time of daily chores for reciting the mantra which could be during riding the bicycle to school or during eating or any other daily activity. Soon you will notice the changes in yourself. There are many success stories related to this mantra. Many people have got the benefits of recitation and there are researches that prove that this mantra is capable of strengthening the will power of a person and many children falling in the Half Life category have turned to the Full Life category. In the next class, we will discuss why a prayer should be taken seriously and given due importance.

Assets :

Inquisitive Questions
1) Which Mantras do you chant daily?
2) What is the significance of Gayatri Mantra?
3) What is the best time and the correct method to recite the Gayatri Mantra?
4) How many times should I chant Gayatri Mantra in a day? What will happen, if I chant less than 100 times?
5) Do you recite Gayatri Mantra silently or loudly? Why?
6) At which stage of life you are? Just introspect and answer.
7) Which stage of life would you like to live and what efforts you need to make to be in that stage?

Interesting Asides
1) Mantras have a great power. Chanting of Mantras can make possible what is considered impossible, otherwise. A dacoit like Valmiki was transformed into a great poet by chanting Rama's name

and later became the author of "Ramayana". He could never pronounce the word "Rama" and instead pronounced it as "Mara".
2) Goddess Parvathi chanted Shiva's name for several years and later got married to Lord Shiva. Sati Savitri could get her husband back from death by chanting Maha Mrityunjaya Mantra.

Suggestive Activity

1) Study a few of the powerful mantras which Hindus generally chant. Write down the significance of each of these mantras. Which of these do you think is most powerful to reduce sins and get closer to God?
2) Chant a mantra of your choice five times before going to sleep.

Day to Day Relevance

Gayatri Mantra is extremely powerful and
- Improves your immunity and focus
- It is a stress buster
- It reduces depression
- Improves the efficiency of your body
- Helps in overcoming the fear of death
- Helps us in maintaining discipline.

We should know the meaning of the Mantras. It needs to be chanted with concentration.

Value Content

Goddess Gayatri is the power of Sun and the mother of Ved. Therefore, Gayatri Mantra is a powerful tool and is like a medicine for cleansing the mind, body and the soul. It also helps us in increasing our concentration and wisdom. When you chant this Mantra, you can feel the positive energy.

Questions to Assess

1) How can you say that Gayatri Mantra is scientific?
2) Does chanting of Gayatri Mantra improve your sixth sense?
3) Can a Christian or a Muslim recite the Gayatri Mantra?
4) Our soul is eternal. Then, what is the use of chanting Gayatri Mantra?
5) What is so special in the Gayatri Mantra, that it is called the supreme mantra?
6) Why is it meant for youth and students specially? (HOT).

Day 11
Namasmarana

In our last class, we had discussed the significance of *Gayatri Mantra*. I would now like to share with you that these classes are beneficial only if you actually practice what you have learnt the way we have discussed. The weightage of the theory (of your learning) is just 5%, whereas the balance 95% weightage is dependent on your practical implementation of the learning. The transformation is a slow process and you may lose patience in this process because you anxiously wait for the instant results. This process is like the homeopathy medicine that has permanent and positive effects and that eradicates the disease from the root, but slowly. It may be a general opinion of the society (including your parents) that this practice is meant only for the senior citizens and that you don't need to indulge into chanting or offering such prayers. But there is a strong need to get involved in such spiritual activities even at your age. Here I would like to advise you that it is going to improve your performance not only academically but also morally and spiritually, if followed judiciously. It will make you a good and a great person in daily life.

We generally think that this is an exercise to be considered after retirement and by that time our habits become so strong that it is not easy to adopt any other practice. Main outcome of this process is :
- gain peace of mind
- increased working capacity and concentration
- improved the attention span
- sharp memory
- more retention power
- more reasoning power

What else does a student require for academic growth! The only thing is that spirituality should not be misused and the power of the mantras should not be taken for granted. One should not expect any miracle to happen or to yield any instant positive result by reciting the mantras without putting in the personal efforts. Always remember that God helps those who help themselves. If we develop the power of discrimination within us, then we will be able to judge between right and wrong even at the crucial age of adolescence. It will also help us to avoid falling prey to the dilemmas that generally students face at this stage. Once you will be able to manage your thoughts, many of your problems will automatically get resolved.

I would like to tell you a story. Once, a child was ploughing a field. While doing so, he found a lamp. The lamp was an antique piece, nearly 5000 years old. When the boy started rubbing the lamp to remove its dust, the lamp started generating the fumes. Suddenly, a genie appeared. The boy got frightened. But the genie assured the boy that he was there to serve him. The genie said, "Do not be afraid of me. Since you are the owner of this lamp, I am your servant. Whatever you order, I will obey you. But my only problem is that I cannot sit idle. If I ever happen to sit idle, I will eat you up." The boy was happy thinking that he would assign a lot of work to the genie to keep him busy. So he ordered the genie to construct a beautiful house for him. He thought that the genie won't find any time to sit idle for at least next 6 months or so. Meanwhile, he would think of another task to be assigned to the genie. But to his surprise, the genie built the house in just one day. The work assigned by the child hardly consumed any time and eventually it became a big problem for the child to think of more tasks that could be assigned to the genie to keep him busy. Now, thinking for the next assignment after such short intervals, became a hard challenge and the boy panicked and ran to his mentor to find out the solution to this problem. The mentor gave him a nice solution. As per the guidance of the mentor, the boy then ordered the genie to erect a pole on the ground and ordered the genie to climb up the pole and come down and continue doing the same till the next task was assigned.

Dear children, I have narrated this story as it symbolizes the nature of the human mind. Our mind is exactly like a genie that can prove as a good servant if we keep it busy. But the moment we spare it free, it starts causing us trouble. Our Mind is like a monkey who is drunk and is bitten by a scorpion. We can tame its movement by Namasamaran only. Namasamaran is a convenient spiritual activity.

You are supposed to keep your mind occupied in one activity or the other. Otherwise an empty mind is considered as a devil's workshop. You can keep yourself busy in many productive activities. Choose any hobby such as gardening, swimming, reading good books etc. You can choose any mantra like Gayatri Mantra (or a short one like *Om Namah Shivaya)* and recite the same in your heart while being engaged in the daily activities like cycling, waiting for someone, bathing, brushing teeth etc., so that your mind does not get any free time to generate useless thoughts. The activity of *Namasamrana* doesn't cost anything and is quite effective too. This is going to remind us of God always. Constant awareness of God will keep you away from all sins and it will be an integrated investment for you. You will enjoy the fruits of this activity during old age too. Your present stage is considered as the habit forming stage and the habits developed at this stage will help you in later due course of your life. Once you get accustomed to *Namsamarna,* you will no longer have any complaints of sleeplessness. If you are waiting for someone, your time will pass easily and the productivity will get a boost by chanting this mantra. You will rejoice in peace and will not get short tempered or impatient while being stuck up in situations like traffic jams or so. You will even enjoy the unpleasant moments of life which otherwise seem lengthy. You will carry a divine glow on your face and everyone will enjoy your company. You will be able to save yourself from useless gossip and sinful acts of speaking ill about others. Again, I am reminding you of 5Ds that we have already discussed. Always remember that you are able to set your priorities as per the duties assigned to you by God. At present, during your student life, your priority should be to gain knowledge and all these methods will supplement to achieve your aim. In the present time, you are mostly under the influence of western culture and you have no courage to share your concerns with others thinking that others will be making fun of you. People now-a-days take pride in proving that there is no such identity as GOD. They ask if God has made us, then who has made GOD. Answers of some of the questions are complicated and you will automatically experience it when you will become an adult.

Assets :
Inquisitive Questions
1) What do you think when you brush your teeth?
2) What is the meaning of "watching the thought"?
3) Have you ever tried to watch your thoughts?
4) What is the role of mind ?
5) Can we tame our mind?
6) How can you stop yourselves from getting stressed and tensed?
7) How can you stop getting negative thoughts that harass you?
8) How can you develop inner peace into a habit?
9) How can you remain calm in stressful situations?
10) Spiritual activities are a boon for all the stages of life i.e. from childhood to old age stage. Justify this statement.

Value Content
If you want success, you should have love for GOD, fear of sin and respect for the law of society. As a student, your duty is to save yourself from bad company.

The ABC of life is "Always Be Careful" and "Avoid Bad Company". The more you have, the more you want, and it is harder to find true happiness and peace of mind.
Rather than trying to fulfil every desire that comes to our mind, we should be content with what we have currently. Currently

contentment does not mean that we should not put any effort to further excel and progress.

Interesting Asides

Remember the story of Rishi Valmiki, who was a dacoit named Ratnakar. He was given the mantra of reciting Ram Ram for self-purification, but when he could not recite RAM RAM. Narada suggested that he should recite MRA MRA. Finally MRA MRA got converted into RAM RAM.

Suggested Activity

- Note down the effects of thinking positive on your relationship with others?
- Make a list of thoughts that came to your mind yesterday. Classify those into positive and negative thoughts.
- Go for Namasmarana for 20 to 30 minutes. After that, list the thoughts that crossed your mind and you enjoyed during the period of Namasamrna. Try this experiment for a week.
- Decide a time interval of about one hour during a day and think only positive during that time interval. Do this for a week and note down the effects.
- Just recite Gayatri Mantra 108 times and note down the time taken by this process.
- Will the exercise of "Namasmarana" help us to live in the present?

Day to Day Relevance

You are to keep your mind occupied in some purposeful activity, but it is observed that whenever you are free, you think of something negative. Occupying yourself with any Mantra will save you from the negativity and will boost your prana level.

Tips to improve the brain power at any age :

- Give your brain a workout
- Exercises
- Laugh

- Eat a brain boosting diet
- Identify things which harm your health
- Silent sitting
- Ditch sugar
- Practise listening

Questions to Assess
1) Will the Namsamrna deviate your attention when you are driving a cycle?
2) Can you watch your thoughts?
3) What is more important - peace of mind or money?
4) What do you mean by the term "unconditionally happy"?
5) Can Silent sitting help in attaining peace of mind?
6) Why is no one completely satisfied with what he has?
7) Name the different spiritual activities.
8) Which name is the most powerful for "Namsamrna" (HOT) ?

Day 12
Contentment

If you ask me, who is richer - the one who has billions of rupees or the one who is contented with what one has, my answer will be the one who is contented. It is not the wealth that decides the richness; it is the happiness on your face that decides where you stand. What is the use of possessions, if it is unable to bring a peaceful sleep for you? In most of the cases, it is observed that people are not happy with what they have, but they are unhappy with what they don't have. Instead of offering their gratitude to GOD for what they have, they are seen grumbling and asking for more possessions, more recognition and more power. The real problem in the world is discontentment. People are not enjoying whatever they have; rather they are just feeling jealous of what others have. Leading a contented life is an art of living and it can only be achieved with the management of your thoughts. If you think that you would be happier when you have a lot of wealth, prosperity and recognition, you are wrong. There is no harm in earning wealth, adding prosperity or getting recognition without using any unfair means and not at the cost of any loss to others. I have observed that you are sad most of the time, not because of the comforts you don't have but because someone else is having more than you. The animals are better than humans as far as contentment is concerned. Once the lion satisfies its hunger, it will not kill anyone else for the next meal in advance.

Dear children, it has been seen that you hard press your parents to purchase a new mobile phone or any other latest electronic gadget, just because your friend is having the same. You do this without even thinking about the financial situation of your parents. You compel your parents to beg, borrow or steal for your desire to acquire a pair of new sports shoes of some branded company, just because your friends have that brand of shoes. At this time, your own comfortable old sports shoes look as if those are of no worth to you. You feel that only after having the new pair of branded sports shoes, will you be the happiest person on the earth. But how temporary is this happiness? You don't realize the sacrifices of your parents for arranging a new pair of shoes for you. Permanent happiness can be achieved by adhering to the contentment. Because of the contentment, you will save lot of energy which otherwise, you are losing by running toward materialistic objects. The same energy can be utilised for your personal growth. Wastage of resources, money and energy should be avoided because it is the cause of your unhappiness. Instead, you should try to taste the "joy of giving" to gain real happiness. If you save some money and spend your savings to help an underprivileged child, it is going to give you permanent happiness. Contentment is the virtue which attracts other persons towards you. A contented person is not jealous of the possessions of others and everyone likes to be a friend of such a person. They can manage themselves under all circumstances. On the contrary, a discontented person gets angry the moment one's desire is not fulfilled. This anger sometimes becomes the reason for many diseases like cancer, high BP and heart disorders. Greed is the sister of discontentment. In fact, a discontented person becomes the prey of all the six vices slowly.

Sometimes we think that if we are content with whatever we have, our growth will cease. Here you are misunderstanding the meaning of "contentment". Contentment is that you work hard to the best of your capacity, enjoy your work and leave the rest to God. You are to compete with yourself only. You should not feel jealous of others and should not try to disrupt the progress of others by using any corrupt practice. Rather, you should take it as a part of the game of life. There are many people who are less fortunate than you are. But that does not mean that you should be satisfied with what you have. Just put your 100% and leave the rest to GOD. One should not confuse contentment with laziness. Laziness amounts to wastage of the talent that GOD has given to you. It is a sin. Sometimes when you do not want to work hard, you try to show that you are content with whatever you have. This is nothing but deceiving yourself. GOD has given you this human birth to work for the best, for your satisfaction and to gain confidence in yourself. You have every right to be discontented with yourself but it should not lead to any jealousy. While playing the game of football, can you tell your teammates that you have not scored another goal because you were contended with whatever the result was? Everyone is sensible enough to understand that this is not contentment and this is something else. One should play the game to the best of one's capability and if the result is still not favourable, then one should not cover it under the carpet of contentment. It should not be taken as a weakness. When you are contented and you still work more, the results will be far better and it will also be beneficial for society.

To explain this further, I will like to share a story with you:
Once there was a Crow who was very satisfied with his life. He used to roam all around happily. One day, he saw a Swan who was pure white in colour. He started thinking that he is black but the swan is so white and that the swan must be the happiest bird in the world. He went to the swan and said, "You must be the happiest bird in the world. You are so white and I am so black that no one likes me". The swan replied, "Actually, I was also feeling that I was the happiest bird alive until I saw a parrot, which has two colours and I think that the parrot is the happiest bird in this world". Now the crow approached the parrot and explained everything.

The parrot explained, "I lived happily until I saw a peacock. I have only two colours but the peacock has many colours". Next, the crow visited the peacock in a zoo and saw that hundreds of people had gathered to see him. After the people left, the crow approached the peacock and said, "Dear peacock, you are so beautiful. Everyday thousands of people come to see you but when someone sees me, he just wants me to move away. I think you are the happiest bird on the planet". The peacock replied sadly, "I always thought that I was the most beautiful and the happiest bird on the planet but due to this beauty, I am entrapped in this cage and sometimes I have even thought to be a crow so that I could happily roam everywhere". The contented person is far richer than a millionaire, because the real worth is peace and not the comforts. Sometimes we think that if we are comfortable, we will be peaceful but it is the vice versa. **Who is happier - a peacock in a cage or a crow in a jungle**?

Sometimes we follow our senses and our senses make us the slave of our mind. Instead, a contented person masters the mind and becomes a master mind. We are tempted to make many mistakes when we are not contented. Someone may ask a question, "If a tennis player is contended with one's achievement, how will one win the game?" Here my counter question to you is, "When will you be a better player, if you concentrate on the ball or if you concentrate on the scoreboard"? I am sure that you will vote for the ball. So contentment is not any hindrance in your progress, rather it facilitates your progress. Many cricket players, because of their efforts to become rich as early as possible, have ruined their future because they were in a hurry to be rich. There are many negative forces ready to catch you when you are progressing.

There are many reasons for discontentment. Main reason is the EGO. We all want that we should be praised, we must be recognised and people should talk about us. To satisfy your ego, you try to show your presence in your own circle by using unfair means. Here some of them work on the principle of ***"Badnam jo honge to kya, naam to hoga"***. The urge to be listened to and to be talked about is there from the infancy stage. Even a small child cries to prove his presence. This is another form of discontentment. During your student life, you should invest in and not invest on. Instead of investing in, we start investing on our clothes, our looks etc. Especially girls waste too much time getting ready to be seen by everyone and when they are not noticed, they become discontented.

Assets :

Inquisitive Questions
1) How happy are people today?
2) Were people happier in the past?
3) How many people are satisfied with their lives in different societies?
4) How do our living conditions affect our satisfaction level?

Interesting Asides

Two friends met in the street. One looked sad and almost on the verge of crying. The other man said, "Hey my friend, how come you look as if the whole world has caved in"? The sad fellow said, "Let me tell you. Three weeks ago, my uncle died and left me 50-thousand dollars."

"That's not bad at all...!"

"Hold on, I'm just getting started. Two weeks ago, an unknown cousin kicked-the-bucket and left me 95-thousand, tax-free to boot."

"Well, that's great! I'd like that."

"Last week, my grandfather passed away and I inherited almost a million."

"So why are they so glum?"

"This week - nothing!"

Suggestive Activity
1) List out the activities from your daily life that give you happiness and satisfaction.
2) Introspect and find out the cause of your discontentment with your achievements or possessions.

Day to Day Relevance

Build relationships with your loved ones, create achievable goals for yourself, and put yourself in situations where you can exercise your personal strengths and abilities; it will help you experience greater feelings of satisfaction. If you can do these things, you can benefit yourself and those around you. Contentment sharpens your thinking process and gives better results of your efforts.

Value Content
1) It is the problem of humans, that we make unnecessary comparisons with others and become sad. We don't value what we have and this tendency leads to the vicious cycle of unhappiness.
2) Secret to happiness is to value what God has given to us and discard the comparison with others.

Questions to Assess
1) Have you ever met a person who is completely satisfied with one's life?
2) Does satisfaction lead to stagnation? How?
3) Does dissatisfaction lead to growth? How?
4) What is satisfaction and how is it different from happiness?

Day 13
Peace of Mind

If you have a magical wand and you are asked for a boon, then what will you ask for? I know that your answers will be quite different. But very few of you will ask for "What you should ask for". The most essential and the most desired boon is the Peace of mind. Surprisingly, now-a-days, peace of mind is missing in most people on the earth. The rich want to be richer. The person having unaccounted money is worried because he/she is afraid of income tax raids and scrutiny. There are many people who are not having even the basic amenities. They are not even getting food for 3 times a day. Their belly is always half full and they are trying hard to make it at least full. Many people are not able to sleep because of several worries in their life. Their quality of sleep is so poor that they are ready to pay anything for a peaceful sleep. People are suffering too much. You should be thankful to God that your position is far better than the persons falling in the two categories described above. You don't have the problem or any tension of a 3 time meal. You are also getting a sound sleep without any worries. Sometimes, it is the task of the parents to wake you up. Your parents are able to provide you with every comfort and therefore, in your present state, the "peace of mind" may not have much value to you. But you will soon realize its importance. In a nutshell, the "peace of mind" is so important for a person that all his other possessions will be of no value in the absence of "peace of mind".

You usually don't value the water in your wash room and continue wasting it, till you come to know that there is no water in the taps. Only when the water stops flowing in the taps, you realise the importance of water. Every elderly person says, "I WANT PEACE", but they do not know who is restricting their peace. It is their "I" and their "WANT". If they remove "I" - that is their EGO and reduce their "WANT" - that is their DESIRE, only "PEACE" will be left. Peace is important for you students because it is your habit developing stage. If you will be peaceful, you will be able to concentrate more and will be more accurate in your work. Haste makes the waste and waste makes the worry. You have to inculcate and develop the habit to start early, drive slowly and reach safely.

Let us now visualise as to why the "peace of mind" is so important in our life. When you get your question paper during an examination, it is advisable to pray and ask God to have your partnership. Instead of starting it fast, it is advisable to read the question paper thoroughly and start writing answers for the questions which you think you are better prepared for. If you are not at peace, there are chances of losing some marks. You will either miss a few questions or write wrong answers somewhere. You will score and get the marks as per your correct answers only. No score would be provided to you for your wrong answers and no one will be able to guess if writing of the wrong answer is consciously done or unconsciously done. For getting peace, you will have to take a few steps.

Of course, you cannot get rid of your desires, but you should have a ceiling on your desires. It is observed that once you see a new mobile phone in your friend's hand, you also start asking for a similar phone from your parents. You think that if you get the new phone, you will be the happiest child on the day you received it. But have you ever noticed how long that happiness stayed with you? You will see that your each desire will give birth to a new desire and if your desire is not fulfilled, your peace will be lost. Better have a ceiling on your desires. Learn to have contentment. For climbing, you have to see up and for walking you will have to see down. There is absolutely no harm in keeping the desire to get a good academic record, but for your other daily needs of roti, kapda and makaan, you should not be that serious. Simple living and high thinking should be your motto. Ensure that your energy is utilised at the right place. Generally it has been observed that you put a lot of pressure on your parents to buy new dresses, new shoes, new gadgets etc. You devote too much of your time to searching for a dress for your farewell party, wasting so much of your precious time. This is the reason why the schools are having a uniform, so that there is no competition of dress/uniform and all children look alike.

Second reason for losing the peace of mind is the disharmony between your thoughts, words and deeds. Generally it is seen that you put yourself into trouble when you lie to someone. And then, to hide one lie, you have to tell many other lies. When you think something, speak something else and do something else, then you put yourself into a mess and your time and energy are wasted. This kind of personality is unable to win the trust of others and unable to have good friends. You will have artificiality around you instead of "heartificiality", which is a new term i.e. you will not find a friend who will be attached to you from the heart. To get the good company of well-wishers, this is an essential quality. You should be trusted in your circle. Only the person who has the harmony of thoughts, words and deeds, is considered trustworthy. When you live in peace, you spread this quality to others as it is contagious. One should try to avoid the company of persons who are not at peace because they will not let you enjoy the peace, as chances of negative vibes from the same cannot help. You must have the company of reliable and peaceful persons.

Another way to have peace is the Prayer. The role of the prayer is similar to the role of shockers of a car. Because of the shockers in a car, you are able to drive on a rough road with ease without any inconvenience to the people in the car. Life itself is a road with so many ups and downs. You are to cross the road with so many pleasures and pains in your life. Prayers make you humble, down-to-earth and also give you the courage. It is because of the absence of the "peace of mind" in a person's life that people are committing suicide, specially the younger ones. The prayers teach patience and perseverance in one's life and this reduces the rate of committing the suicide. One must learn that this is the reason why we go for prayers in the morning. This should not be just a ritual and you must learn to pray and ask God to give you all peace, which at present, is missing from your life.

Assets :
Inquisitive Questions
1) Presence of every comfort is surety for peace of mind and vice versa. Do you agree? Why?
2) Do you progress more in the presence of "peace of mind" or in the absence of "peace of mind"? Why?
3) What are the factors responsible for peace of mind?
4) When will you have peace of mind - when you are busy in work or when you are sitting idle?
5) How far do you agree with the statement – "If you want to be happy, make someone else happy"?
6) Explain the meaning of contentment as used in this lesson.

Suggestive Activity
You are a rich person and you go to attend the birthday party of your employee's son. You find him having more "peace of mind" than you have. How will you react? Do a role play with a minimum of two people. You may add some more members of the employee's family.

How does the habit of "start early, drive slowly and reach safely" can help you in your studies and personality development? Illustrate with examples.

Interesting Asides
The "per capita income", comforts and lifestyle are much better in the USA as compared to our country. Yet, the suicidal rate in USA is more than ours.

Day to Day Relevance

Comfortable and peaceful are two different things. You can be comfortable but not peaceful and vice versa. The best way to gain peace of mind is to reduce your desires. If you enjoy your duty, you will be comfortable and peaceful.

Value Content

If we want peace of mind, we should not go for the policy of "get and forget" but we should adopt the principle of "give and forgive".

Questions to Assess

1) Do you think that your progress will cease if you will have peace of mind? Why?
2) Why do you lose your peace of mind when you keep expecting the result of our work?
3) Should we make our expectation level zero if we want peace of mind? Why?
4) What are the reasons for losing the peace of mind?
5) What is the importance of peace of mind for a student?
6) What do you mean by ceiling on desires?
7) Is the ceiling on desire an obstacle in your progress? Explain why.
8) Is there any difference between contentment and peace of mind (HOT)?

Day 14
Love of God, Fear of Sin and Respect for the Law of Society

The topic of our today's lesson is "Love of God, Fear of Sin and Respect for the Law of Society". We will take each of these aspects one by one. We should love God because God is our supreme father but unfortunately we do not love God and we consider God is there only to catch and punish us for doing something wrong. Sometimes, we carry the same impression for our parents too. Some even do not believe that God is any reality. They have different questions over the existence of God like :

-    If God has made us then who has created God?
-    If God is there then why are there sufferings and miseries in life?
-    If God is present in me then why and how do I commit sin?
-    How is God so partial that one gets riches and the other one struggles so hard even to make both ends meet?

To understand the game of life and the concept of God, I will take the example of the water cycle since you are all familiar with this phenomenon. Consider the ocean as God. From time to time, some ocean water turns into vapours and forms clouds. Then these clouds turn into water drops and fall upon us in the form of rain. Drops of water fall at different places. These water drops turn into different shapes and different forms and ultimately take the shape of a river to go back to merge into the ocean again. The journey of each water drop is different. Some drops take a longer time to reach back to the ocean and the others take comparatively less time. The only difference between water cycle and human cycle is that water can merge with sea without any condition of purity but for a human being, there is a condition to merge with the Almighty. The condition is that our subconscious mind should be as pure as it was while emerging from God.

To make the game more interesting, human beings are given free will to act and use the power of discrimination as per their own choice. So man is the creator of his own destiny. If he acts according to the systems prescribed by God in the religious books (Vedas for Hindus, Quran for Muslims, Bible for Christians and so on), he can merge with God easily. But if he gets attracted towards sensory pleasures, he gets attached with the world and suffers as per his karmas. Attachment with the world is the detachment from God and detachment from the world is attachment with God. Each one of us has to go through the good or bad phases of life according to our own karmas of this birth and the previous births. We all have the capacity to become God provided we understand the concept. Nothing new is to be done. No need to put on the saffron clothes or to carry out any rituals. We are only supposed to do our duties in the best possible manner, keeping in mind that only our righteous deeds will please God. Now tell me, can you make God happy by making your parents happy, by helping ever and hurting never, by loving and serving all? To check if you have made God happy or not, God has given you a super conscious mind. So, God is not to be blamed for any of your miseries. God is someone whom we should love. Keep your CIA (Constant Integrated Awareness) activated. It means that whatever you are doing, God is watching.

2nd aspect is the Fear of Sin. Again the question is what is a sin? Answer to this question is simple. All our thoughts or actions that are not pleasing God, can be considered as sin. All the following actions will fall in the category of sins :

- you are hurting someone
- you are not helping any one
- you are not loving all the creatures of God
- you are not serving the ones that come your way
- you are using the natural resources for your selfish gain
- you are not paying back your share of service

To judge and decide as to what should be considered as sin and what should not be, you can use the power of your super conscience, provided you are willing to listen to its call. Your super conscious mind has self-esteem that keeps guiding you if you ask for it. Once you start ignoring the super conscious mind, it becomes dormant. It generally happens because you want to please your senses that give you momentary pleasures. We generally can't discriminate between the temporary and the permanent pleasures. This is a game. Ultimately you have to merge with God but only if you play your game honestly and be careful about the role that God has assigned you. Then only, this game will be pleasurable, otherwise it is going to give you pain. Fear of sin will keep bothering and disturbing you if you continue hurting others, cheating others and getting pleasure in making fun of others. Your next birth will be destined accordingly. You may take birth in slum areas with less privileged parents. You don't know what kind of sins you have committed in your previous births that God has not revealed to you. But you are placed accordingly. You are fortunate that in this birth your placement shows that your previous karmas were good. You should keep on doing righteous tasks in this birth too.

The 3rd aspect is the respect for the law of society. How to enter the world with respect for the law of society is given to all in the form of a manual. This law itself is a charter and a plan to guide us on what is to be done and what is not to be done. But here too, God has provided us with EGO to make the game interesting. The urge to get recognised, to look beautiful, to have more comforts in comparison to the people around you, your big 'I' compels you to go for short cuts. You get so engrossed in enjoying the worldly pleasures and you start thinking that the purpose of this life is just to please the senses. While taking shortcuts and breaking the law of society, you ignore the presence of God and start ignoring your super conscious mind too. This is how you prepare the ground for the next birth and a day comes in every one's life when a person feels that 'I Want Peace'. But one does not know that it is the 'I' and 'Want' which restrict one to get peace. Once you remove 'I' and have a ceiling on 'Want', you get contended with whatever possessions you have and thereby automatically attain peace. Life is a game and you have been given a role by God and your role changes as per your age. Sometimes you are to perform the role of a son or a daughter, a father, a mother, a friend, a grandfather or a grandmother etc. Let's perform our role to the best of our capabilities so that the Director i.e. the God may give you a better role next time than what we have got in this life. So to improve upon, we have to compete with ourselves only. Teaching manual is there and the Prompter/Mentor too is there to guide you. But one needs to put in one's own efforts.

Assets :

Inquisitive Questions
1) Have you ever noticed the existence of God ? When and How?
2) Do you feel inner sin or repentance if you ever steal cash or jewellery from your own house to buy an expensive gift for your girlfriend?
3) Do you ever feel sin or guilty when you bunk school and go to watch a movie?
4) How do you feel, when you help others without expecting anything in return?

Suggestive Activity

Keep a spiritual diary and devote ten minutes to introspect the day's activities.

Value Content

Believe in GOD, believe in Karma theory and get rid of the fear of sin. Listen to your conscience – it will always prick you whenever you attempt to do something wrong or harm someone. Be Empathetic always.

Day to Day Relevance

You will notice that whenever you ignore the pricks from your conscience and go on doing wrongful acts, you are under constant attack of the fear of sin. Also, sooner or later, you start repenting when you yourself face the same wrong with yourself. Whenever you try to challenge the existence of God, something happens in your life that you are forced to believe otherwise.

Interesting Asides

A similar lesson has been given by lord Buddha. His lesson was *"budham sharnam gacchami"* (love for GOD). *"Dharmam sharnam gacchami"* (fear of sin), *"sangham sharanam gacchami"* (respect for the law of society). It is the English translation of *dev priti, pap bhiti* and *sangh niti* by Sri Sathya Sai Baba.

Questions to Assess

1) What is worth learning from this lesson?
2) Is "Fear" a sin?
3) There have been cases where the son of an influential politician attacks people (or rapes girls) and runs away thinking that no law can punish him. Is "Law of Society" not for him or will he be tried under the defined laws of society?
4) What can you do to get the love of God?
5) Is there any connection of love for God, fear of sin and respect for the law of society? (HOT)

Day 15
Harmony of Thoughts, Words and Deeds

Although we have already discussed the importance of harmony of thoughts, words and deeds in life, let us discuss in detail why we should have such harmony. What is the meaning of having harmony of thought, words and deeds? You must have seen people around you owning a dual character. They preach something. But their actions do not reflect what they preach, when they get stuck in a similar situation. Their attitude and behaviour pattern is entirely different. Many of our politicians are leading an artificial life. They think something, speak something and do something else. Harmony is - whatever we think, speak and do - all are aligned to each other. Unless we practice such harmony, it is sure that we cannot have peace in our life. Our life will be stressful and we won't be able to have a sound sleep. It leads to lack of alertness and low productivity at the workplace too. Inefficiency in your work often leads to frustration. This is going to add more stress and a never ending negative chain gets formed.

Let us understand as to why people are not having harmony of thoughts, words and deeds. We are living in a competitive world. Our ego wants to show off our possessions and intelligence to our acquaintances and we want to prove that we are leading a better life in comparison to others. With these tendencies in mind, we hide many things from others and create some sort of artificiality. In fact it takes too much effort to prove something which is false or doesn't exist at all. We do it deliberately just to nurture our ego. We want others to feel that we are wiser, richer and smarter than them. The other people also follow the same because they too have to cater to their ego. In fact, instead of competing with our own self, we feel pleasure in proving ourselves superior to others. This creates jealousy amongst each other. Our actions followed by reactions start forming a negative circle. It results in building up an unhealthy atmosphere around us with one thought in our mind — "Everything is fair in love and war". We eventually start considering life as a war instead of considering it a game. With this unhealthy spirit of competition, the result is that instead of making our own line bigger, we start erasing the lines of others to show that our line is bigger than theirs.

Whenever we introspect and find that we are under stress, major chances are that we think something else, speak something else and do something else. Imagine what will be the position of a chariot, when it is being pulled by 3 horses in different directions! Imagine the speed of a chariot when all the 3 horses are running in the same direction with the same speed. We should do good, see good and be good. It is possible only when there is harmony of thoughts, words and deeds. We must keep a vigil on our acts. The chances of our acts being pure will be remote if there is no harmony. Once the unity and the purity are missing, the chances of work being divine are extremely bleak.

A stressful life gives birth to several diseases like Heart problem, Blood Pressure, Cardiac problem and indigestion etc. God has given us this life to enjoy but when we do not take harmony seriously, we lose the charm in life by getting involved in desire, anger, greed, attachment, ego and jealousy. Negativity is dangerous for everyone, be it a child or an adult. Keep your thoughts pure and selfless and your life should be purposeful and simple. It should be an open book. Gratitude and sacrifice should be your priorities. People should enjoy your company. Once your thoughts, words and deeds are in harmony and your thoughts are scrutinised by the super conscious mind, you will automatically be accepted by society. But a question arises- "What about a dacoit who is thinking of robbery and is proud of his profession"? He speaks and gets involved in the same activities. Will he be peaceful? Yes, he is convinced but it's not possible that his super conscious mind also approves his thoughts. So one thing is certain that harmony of negative thoughts, words and deeds is not possible because we are living in a civilized world and it is difficult to go against the laws of society.

Theoretically we know that there should be harmony between thoughts, words and deeds. Still it is seen that most people cannot do it. Who is preventing them from doing so? It is their mind (that is the sum total of their five senses plus past life experiences). Over use and unfair use of the five senses is responsible for the disharmony. Our mind, the generator of thoughts under the influence of five senses, seeks pleasure through any means, may be even unfair. But thinking that our intentions should not be known to the public, we want to hide the same by saying something else. Here starts the disharmony between thoughts and deeds. Both thoughts and words are the powerful lions. In this fight of two lions, the winner is the one, whom we feed more and hence our action is the outcome of any of the two (or sometimes even different from both of these). Our action prompted by one of the two, depends upon the feeding done by us. But if the action is something different, it creates more confusion, our whole personality divides into several parts and as a result, the "peace of mind", which is essential, gets disturbed. It is a kind of chain reaction. If there is disharmony in thoughts, words & deeds, it is certain that our subconscious mind is going to be impure. More impurities will lead to worldly attachment and the person will have to pay for his karmas, either in this lifetime or in the next birth.

Assets :

Inquisitive Questions

1) Have you ever noticed that your mood is off and you do not know its reason? When you come to know the reason, you are able to set the mood?
2) Which is more important-peace or comfort? Justify the answer.
3) Do you think that you can always hide your intention by your words?
4) Which is more powerful - thought, word or deed?

Suggestive Activity

Just try to show calmness on your face, when you are angry?

Sit silently and visualise the situation when your mood is bad. Is there any situation of disharmony of thoughts, words and deeds?

Interesting Asides

While making a movie, the director of the film tries to make his/her actor angry by some act so that the shot looks natural. Similar act is tried for a sad scene too.

Value Content

- Unity of thoughts, words and deeds brings purity and purity is the virtue of man. It is easier for a person with unity to be divine.
- Purity of mind develops power of intuition, reasoning, fearlessness, patience and many other qualities relevant to your success.

Day to Day Relevance

You will observe that a teacher with unity of thoughts, words and deeds is liked by children and even remembered after schooling too.

Questions to Assess

1) Is it possible to keep harmony of thoughts, words and deeds, in today's world? Why?
2) Can you name a few people who had kept harmony of thoughts, words and deeds throughout their life? How was their life, according to you?
3) What do you understand by "Harmony of thoughts, words and deeds"?

Day 16
Time Management

In our previous classes, we have discussed the functioning of the mind. We have reached the conclusion that an empty mind is the devil's workshop. In order to make a child learn discipline, a plan should be chalked out in such a way that the children hardly get any time to idle away. It should be assured that the students are occupied the whole day and hardly get any time to waste. Their mind should generate only two types of thoughts i.e.

(1) how to participate in the activities assigned to them.

(2) how to complete those particular activities on the stipulated time.

Time is one of the most important resources that help us in grooming our life. God has granted us 1440 minutes per day. Not even a single minute can be carried forward from these 1440 minutes a day. These minutes are to be invested on the same day. But you will find many people wasting these minutes or using it in different ways. Many accomplished individuals struggle to find enough time for adequate rest. They generally have targets to achieve and try to maximize their output by making the maximum use of the time in hand. People remember them because of their hard work and deeds. You might have seen many people sitting in the sun, playing cards all day long, without any constructive work in their hand. If questioned about their activities, their typical response would be "Just passing time." A day comes when time reverts back and erases them from history. They no longer exist. Life is invaluable and isn't bestowed by a higher power simply for passing the time. Time is a precious gift given by God which needs to be utilised fruitfully. The main characteristic of time is that it flows like a river in forward direction and can never flow backward. Wasting of time, that too during a student life, is worse than a sin. But I wish that we all have a common understanding on this issue. What should be considered as wastage of time?

For time management, divide the day (24 hours) into four parts (generally unequal) and place the tasks/activities in the four quadrants (categories) as per their importance and urgency on that particular day.

First category tasks placed in the 1st quadrant are of the category that is quite **"Urgent as well as Important"**. You are going to appear in your final exams and your exam is starting after an hour. It takes approximately 50 minutes to reach the examination centre. So, you start immediately from home as it is urgent and important to reach the centre. You happen to cross an accident site, where a person is lying helplessly on the road. Now shifting him to hospital is urgent and important. Likewise, attending an interview for a good job, going to a doctor (in case you aren't feeling well) and going to the podium for your lecture when your name is announced, are all urgent as well as important tasks. Therefore, urgent work must not be delayed. If such tasks are delayed, there are chances to suffer a loss. If there is no loss in delaying a task, then that task is not appropriate to be categorised as "Urgent and important". Most intelligent people try to plan in such a way that minimum work is placed in the first category. These wise people try to place their work in the second category.

Second category is of the tasks that are **"Important but not Urgent"**. You feel that you need a dental check-up, you plan a visit to the dentist and take an appointment. This task is important but not so urgent. But it may become urgent if you keep postponing your visit to the dentist. Your class teacher has assigned you some work on Wednesday. Now her next class will be on Monday. In spite of having enough time in hand, you decide to finish the work on the same day. But if you wait till Sunday, then by that time, the work will be shifted to category one. i.e. it will become "Urgent as well as Important". Let's take another example. Suppose your bathroom tap is leaking slightly. To call the plumber and get it repaired immediately, is the task that comes under this category but if you procrastinate, the time will come when the problem goes beyond repair and you will have to replace the tap. So, working on the second category and not being allowed to convert any assignment of 2nd category to the first one, is a sign of wisdom. It is well said 'Stitch in time saves nine'.

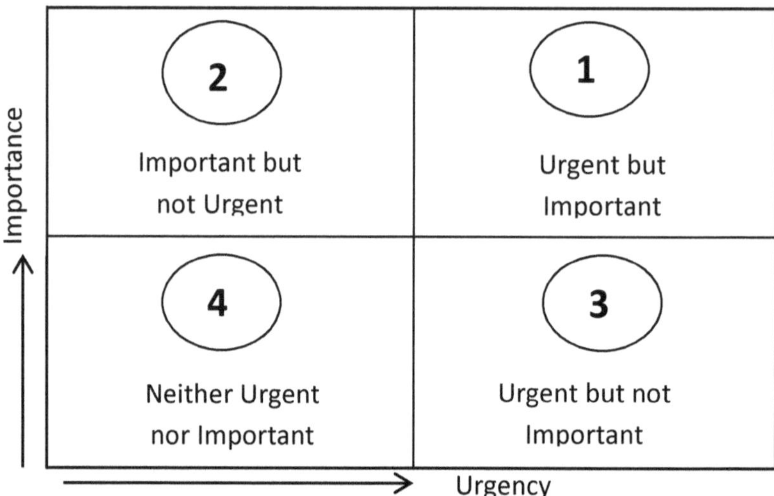

Third category is of the tasks that are **"Urgent but not Important"**. Suppose you are addicted to any TV show which is about to begin, then coming near the TV and waiting for the programme is urgent but watching the same show is not at all important. Once you skip watching any show, you should not feel bad. We can easily avoid the tasks of this category. Your friend has invited you to witness a cricket match which is about to begin within half an hour. This may be urgent but not important. Usually such kind of work can be easily skipped and a lot of wastage of time can be avoided.

The fourth category is the one with all such tasks that are **"Neither Urgent and Nor Important"**. Gossiping on the phone with your friends, going through junk mails and texting through WhatsApp are the kind of tasks that can be avoided. Present generation is spending most of their valuable time doing activities that come under this category. This is one of the reasons that their work in the 1st and 2nd category suffer. You are advised to check the percentage of time you devote for 3rd and 4th category quadrants. It's always recommended to maintain a diary and keep a check on the total amount of time consumed in different activities that fall in each category quadrant. I am sure that you will be surprised to note the amount of time that you are devoting on the activities that come under category 3 and 4. You will have to plan. Your maximum time should be spent for category 2 and avoid it to shift to category 1. When category 2 activities are shifted to category 1, the quality of work suffers and a lot of tension gets built up. When there is tension, it gives birth to a number of other problems and affects our health too. Sometimes the results are very bad. Suppose you start late from your house and try to catch a train and in hurry, your foot slips while boarding the train. You suffer tremendously. Therefore, it is always recommended that you should start early, drive slowly and reach safely.

You can keep a strict watch on your activities and find out the reason for your time being wasted. One of the most common problems with you is that you don't stack your belongings at a proper place, in an organised way. Usually a lot of your precious time gets wasted in searching for your things. Before going to school, you search for your socks because you don't put them at the place that is meant for the same. Likewise, you search for your stationery items and other small stuff and your lot of time gets wasted. So, now onwards, take a pledge that you will place your belongings at the fixed designated places after their use. This doesn't mean that the time you spend with your parents, friends, and relatives should be categorized solely as either category 3 or category 4 task. Doing work smartly is more important than working hard. Time wasted is life wasted. If today you waste your time, tomorrow the time will ruin you and someone else will take your place.

Each work should be given its due importance. But this should not be an excuse to avoid some important tasks. Doing work at the right time and at the right place also saves your time. How do you find out where your time has gone? You can maintain a time log, recording all activities undertaken within specific intervals, say every 30 minutes throughout the day. Jot down everything you do, whether productive or not, to keep track of your time usage. The time log could be like the one illustrated below :

<table>
<tr><td colspan="4" align="center">Time Log
Date : xx/xx/xx</td></tr>
<tr><td>Serial No.</td><td>Start Time</td><td>Description of Activities</td><td>Duration</td></tr>
<tr><td></td><td></td><td></td><td></td></tr>
</table>

This time log can be used to analyse where you have wasted the time, who has interrupted you, how much of the day it was in your control, which tasks could have been avoided (or postponed) and how much you have achieved against your plan for the day.

If you interview an officer and a labourer, you will find that the former had respected the time during his childhood and during his school time, he was conscious about his future but the labourer was not. Once the time is wasted, it cannot be recovered at a later stage and then there is no use of repenting of your foolishness.

Assets :
Inquisitive Questions
1) You are given 24 hours a day, like every other person. What percentage of it would you like to spend on your studies in a day?
2) What should be the right time to get up in the morning?
3) How much time should be spent on sleeping?

4) Why should we manage the time? What will happen if you do not manage it?
5) What do you understand about "Time Management"?
6) Why do we say that time wastage is life wasted?

Suggestive Activity

1) List different activities that you have to take up for the next day. Classify those into four categories explained above and assign time to these activities. Now analyse the extent you were able to stick to your plan. List the reasons for any deviation. Try this experiment for a week.

2) Do not keep the objects (books, keys, shoes etc.) at the same place, from where you have picked them up, after their use. Instead, replace their places. Study the effect of it on the time saved, stress level, behaviour with others etc. Try this experiment for a week and then note down any changes in you.

3) Write a diary for a month and keep a record of the time spent on every kind of work you carry out. Just check about the time that you have spent on productive work? Was there any scope of spending more time on productive work?

Value Content

If you want to know the value of a year, just ask the child who failed.

If you want to know the value of a month, ask the farmer, who delayed planting by one month.

If you want to know the value of a day, just ask the student, who was declared overage by one day only.

If you want to know the value of an hour, ask a student, who couldn't complete his exam because of paucity of time.

If you want to know the value of a minute, ask the person who missed the train because of the delay by a minute.

If you want to know the value of a second, ask the runner who missed the gold medal because of a fraction of a second.

Interesting Asides

The word "management" itself contains the answer, one who can manage men and t(time). Management= Manage+ men+t

Day to Day Relevance

Usually it is observed that time cares for those who care for the time. God has given the same amount of time to everyone, but how to utilise the time is in your own hands. You must have seen that one who adheres to time, keeps a diary in their pocket & fixes priorities accordingly.

Questions to Assess

1) What per cent of time can be saved, by placing the right thing at the right place?
2) Give an example of a situation where we generally shift from "important but not urgent" to "important and urgent".
3) Is there any way to postpone today's time to tomorrow?
4) "Sada swasth raho, vyast raho aur mast raho" (be healthy, busy, and without worry). How far is this statement a blessing?
5) Plan today's time table as a part of the time management exercise.
6) How far do you agree to the statement : "Remaining busy is also a mantra to be happy." (HOT)

Day 17
Values

Topic for the day is **'Values'**. Before we proceed further, let us understand the meaning of 'Value'. Every object has a value, which makes the object worthy e.g. Ice has a value of coolness. If any object that we name as Ice but is not cool, we will not consider it as ice. Similarly, the value of coal is hot. Do not misunderstand the word "property" with "value". You might think that coolness is the physical property of ice and hotness is the physical property of coal. You will differentiate between the words ``property'' and "value" as we learn more in this class. There are certain values that only exist in human beings which make the human beings distinct from other species on the planet such as animals, plants and other living and non-living things. When the values, which are the paramount characteristics of a human being, are not present in a person, we cannot classify that person as a human being.

If we search Google for the list of human values, we will find that there are approximately 434 values. Values are universal in nature. We cannot categorize them as Indian values or Western values etc. Although the list of values is quite big, we shall put them into 5 main categories. Rest of the values are considered as Sub values. The main values are- Truth, Righteousness, Peace, Love and Non-violence.

The question of "Why should we adhere to these values?" is akin to the inquiry posed to a football player, which is "Why should we have rules and regulations to play football?" To play the game of life safely, values are the charter that we must adhere to. It may vary a little from religion to religion but the basics are the same for all. Let us discuss each value one by one.

1. **Truth** - Lie has speed but truth has stamina. Value of Truth is one of the most required values for the students. Truth deals with the insightful aspects of education. Value of truth is not confined only to speaking the truth and not to tell lies. It contains curiosity and the knowledge of distinguishing between temporary and permanent. What is your purpose in life? All the questions that one must ask to satisfy our intelligence, forms a part of Truth. The domain of Truth includes:
   - our ability to stand firm when our conscience tells us that we are right.
   - finding out the reason for every action we perform.
   - experimenting and knowing what is right.
   - ability to know what is going to stay permanently with us.

2. **Righteousness** - One should perform one's duties and put one's heart and soul into it. We are supposed to adhere to the rules and regulations of the society. We are all aware of the general Do's and Don'ts. Our Vedas have already laid down a system about what to eat and what not to eat, how to behave with youngsters and how to behave with elders and so on. Though the norms are clear, yet if you have any confusion, you can take the help of your super conscious mind. We often term it as Soul or Antaratma etc. We want independence in our lives. We often say, "It is my life and I will do whatever I wish". Independence works only with responsibility. But we want independence without any responsibility towards self or the society. We follow the path to satisfy our senses only. Sometimes, we go up to any extent, without even bothering about the side effects of the same. There is no limit. But I must say that the real independence is the inner dependence. We must depend upon our inner consciousness. We'll then automatically realise that our desires will not trouble us. The actual independence is when we are sure of our conduct and *Dharmas*. When we follow our karmas, other values naturally develop alongside. The Geeta serves as an excellent guide on righteousness, teaching us to fulfil our duties and entrust the rest to God.

3. Peace – It is the most desirable value. Everyone wants Peace but we generally try to find it outside. People think that they will achieve peace once they satisfy the hunger of their senses. But nobody can ever satisfy one's hunger. One who is contended in his life is the most peaceful person on the earth. The greatest barrier to finding peace is often our own ego. In our pursuit, we compete with others, believing that surpassing our neighbours in wealth, outshining our friends in appearance, or being healthier than others will bring peace. Though these aspects matter, the pursuit of superiority and ego prevents us from truly resting in peace. While competing with others, we sometimes miss the real happiness. Instead of being thankful to God for what we have, we strive hard to possess what we don't have. Peace can never be attained by acquiring worldly pleasures. It develops from inside. When we are appreciated, we become happy but on the other hand, we feel bad when criticized. It means that we have handed over our control system to someone else. To acquire peace, we need to adhere to the attitude of same feelings in pleasure and pain or in gain and loss. When we put our heart and soul to achieve a goal and reach to the destination we have fixed, imagine the amount of peace we get. We must take both as the blessings from God as a situation to learn.

4. Love – It is the binding force. It is because of love that this universe is sustaining. As per Newton's law of gravitation, everybody is attracting other bodies. Several examples of the same can be seen in the universe. It is because of the same love that planets are moving around the sun and maintaining a fixed discipline. Love with worldly things is termed as "Attachment". But the same love with God is termed as "Devotion". Love adds beauty to life. It is because of the love that we are having a well-balanced family. Love takes on various forms: patriotism for one's homeland, an affair for the opposite sex, and the purest form found in a mother's love. A mother's affection for her children stands as one of the greatest expressions of love, rivalled only by the love of God. Love manifests differently: in words as truth, in action as righteousness, in feeling as peace, and in understanding as non-violence.

5. Last but not the least, is the value of **Non-violence**. It is the most essential requirement for a civilised world. Live and let live is the motto of non –violence. It is relevant to everyone, irrespective of age, caste, colour, creed, race or gender. Non-violence in thought is not to have ill feelings for others and not to feel jealous of others. It is commonly observed that people are not sad because of their own discomforts but they are unhappy to see the comforts of others. Jealousy, having grudges for others and ego are the ingredients that cause violence of thoughts. Wastage and pollution of natural resources like water, air and coal also fall under the category of violence. Therefore we must make sincere attempts to avoid the misuse of natural resources. If you are wasting, you are taking someone else's share. Hence it is against the maxim 'Live and let live'. We have enough for our 'Need' but not for our 'Greed'. If we want to reduce the pollution of noise, air and water, we will have to adopt the principles of non-violence.

We cannot have any water tight compartment for values. Once we start taking care of one value, the other values will automatically be taken care of. We can be called humans in real sense only if we take care of our values system. Once we appreciate the values, our quality of life will surely improve. Life is a game and values are certain parameters to play that game. Once we take care of these parameters, we will make less fouls and will win the game cheerfully.

Assets :
Inquisitive Questions
1) Which religion emphasizes most on the five main values i.e. Truth, Righteousness, Peace, Love and Non-violence?
2) What are your family values?
3) How do you define a traditional family and the traditional values?

4) Why non-violence is considered to be essential for a civilised society?

Interesting Asides

You prepare coffee to drink. The value of a coffee cup is the coffee in it. There are some other ingredients like sugar, milk, water etc. and these ingredients can be less or may be absent. But if the coffee from the drink is absent, it will no longer be named as coffee. So the value is something which is a must and defines an object or a person. Main value of a coffee cup is coffee, rest are the sub values.

Interestingly there are 343 values which make a person a real human. Out of 343 values, five are the main values.

Suggestive Activity

1) Find out the situation where there is a conflict of values.
   Some of the situations are given below to ease your work.
   (a) In Mahabharata, Yudhistra was asked to say that "Ashawthama is dead". He was aware that it was about an elephant and not the man and he was also aware of the purpose of such an announcement.
   (b) Rama left Sita on the comments of a washerman, though he was aware of the truth.
   (c) Rama killed Bali by attacking on his back which is considered hypocrisy.
2) You have studied five main values. Which is the easiest for you to follow out of these five values? Follow it (the easiest one) religiously for a week and observe its effect on the other four values.

Day to Day Relevance

Life without values is like a football match without any rule and regulation.

Value Content

VALUE determines the worth of a person, opportunity, task, time, situation and relations. Besides 5 main values described in this lesson, Discipline, Justice, Respect, Honesty and Prudence are 5 other values that should not be ignored. It is the values that teach you the real meaning of life.

Questions to Assess
1) What do you value most in your life now and why?
2) Have your values changed with your age, environment and your company?
3) Would you sacrifice your values for your job or to get a promotion?
4) Do you consider "Hard Work" as an important Value? Why?
5) Can we classify Value as Indian Value or American Value or are the Values same everywhere?
6) Which Value is responsible for Earth to move around the sun?
7) Does non-violence mean that we have to passively accept injustice?
8) Should we tell lies, if it benefits someone? (HOT)

Day 18
Personality

Today we will discuss about a very important topic i.e. **"Personality"**. It can be split into two words – "person + capability" or "person + utility". Personality is not only the dress and the outer appearance or the beauty of an individual. It has a broader perspective. If personality has something to do with the dress or the outer appearance then Gandhi Ji would not have been so famous. Personality is considered as the sum total of your internal and external traits. Outer personality can attract someone, but the inner personality is necessary to maintain a relationship. Therefore, it is important to develop the inner personality. We generally use our precious time to refine our outer appearance only and seldom show any concern about the inner self. This is the basic difference between western countries and India. According to our culture, we put more stress on developing the strength of our inner self whereas the western culture gives more weightage to the outer appearance only. They have specific dress codes for different functions. Over a period of time, we have started imitating them mindlessly. Earlier we used to be least bothered about fancy dresses or the outer appearance. Of course, beauty is God gifted and cannot be ignored. But the outer beauty is not everything that one has. To make a personality meaningful, many other aspects are to be considered. You have to give prime importance to your inner personality.

Before we proceed further with our discussion on how to develop inner personality, let us first understand the reasons for the differences in our inner and outer personalities. We can categorize our negative behaviour into six main aspects of negativity, which are:
-    the desire for sex (kaam)
-    anger (krodh)
-    greed (lobh)
-    attachment (moh)

- ego (ahankar)
- jealousy (irshya)

These six negative traits are viewed as natural instincts inherited from our animal origins, as before evolving into humans, we were predominantly animals. Though we're unaware of our past human lives, the animalistic tendencies from which we emerged as humans still persist within us. Each animal is known for a different kind of trait i.e. a lion is known for aggression, a donkey for laziness, a fox for cleverness, a dog for greed and so on. The six negative traits are seen as instincts inherited from our animal origins, as our earlier existence predominantly resembled that of animals before evolving into humans. Despite our lack of awareness about past human lives, the animalistic tendencies that facilitated our evolution into humans continue to exist within us.

Out of these six vices, one or two are prominent in us and rest are present in some traces only. It's quite rare to find any one individual who is having all the six vices in abundance. Its vice versa is also true. To develop the inner personality, we will have to first introspect and realize the negative traits present in us. Minor negativities can be controlled by adhering to the discipline but to overcome the prominent vices, determination and proper planning is required. For getting rid of these vices, we'll have to go through the sequence of 4Fs that has already been discussed.

Besides getting rid of the negativity, we have to raise the quality of positivity in us. These positive traits are named as values. Mainly we can put them into five categories:
- truth (sathya)
- righteousness (dharam)
- peace (shanti)
- love (prem)
- non-violence (ahimsa)

We will discuss these values one by one. If we plan to raise the level of these values, we'll have to start working consistently and that too as early as possible. Otherwise it is going to become an integral part of our nature and will further affect the process of refinement of our inner personality. Adopting these values is the purpose of human life and the people who adopt these values in their life are remembered even after their death. There is another world beyond this materialistic world, where such people are given their due place. No one can carry money, valuable possessions or fame to that world. Only our good deeds will accompany us there. Therefore, to develop the inner personality, service to mankind is an important tool. By helping the underprivileged, one can easily raise the quality of positivity in oneself. In fact this life and this body is provided to us for this purpose only. *'Propakaram Idam Shareeram'* i.e. this body is meant to serve others. With proper care and introspection, we can raise the level of positivity and lower the level of negativity in us. Ultimately when the inner personality is developed, it gets reflected through our face too. There is a glossy look on the faces of the persons who adhere to these values.

It is not necessary to work upon all your negativities at a time. You can always start with any one and you will find that other negativities also reduce to some extent. Present trend is to "invest on" and not to "invest in". "Invest on" is a costly and temporary affair but "invest in" is cheap, permanent and trustworthy. If you develop your inner personality and keep the company of like-minded people, it is sure that you will be peaceful. You will save a lot of your time and energy and you will be successful in life. You make yourself presentable and no one is against this. You should wear good, clean clothes, keep yourself clean, be always in high spirits with a smiling face and greet your fellow beings with enthusiasm. Keep doing regular exercises, avoid junk food and go according to the laws of healthy living. Nobody can underestimate the importance of the outer personality, but you are not to ignore your inner personality too. It matters a lot as to how you deal with others. If you have the tendency to help others, if you are not hurting anyone and if you are loving and serving all, then only you are a perfect human being. No one likes selfish people. Very soon they are exposed in society. A positive inner personality is the future. It will save you from the vices.

Assets :
Inquisitive Questions
1) Can Personality change? How, When and Why?
2) Could climate change affect someone's personality?
3) How would you rate Openness, Nervousness and Socialness as part of one's personality?
4) How do you distinguish between internal and external traits in someone's personality?
5) Do internal traits convey more of your personality than the external traits?

Suggested Activity
1) You know each student in your class, each teacher in your school and each of your family members. Think more about them and try to write down the positive traits of any 10 of them. Also, ask your friends to write about your traits and then exchange what you have written about them and what they have written about you.

2) Enlist your negative traits and positive traits. Classify the negative traits in order of their ease of removal i.e. from easy to difficult (to remove). Try to make these less effective with proper efforts.

Value Content
Get rid of your negative inner traits and cultivate more positive traits. Animal instinct will lead you nowhere. Outer appearance is momentary. It is more important to develop the inner personality.

Day to Day Relevance

Most of the time, you are with your classmates, friends, teachers and family members. Your actions and gestures in school, home, office meetings or elsewhere convey a lot about your personality. So, be cautious of your actions and gestures.

If you are having any of the negative inner traits and you keep yourself unaware of this fact, you will earn a bad name and people will run away from you. You will lose friends and relatives. Try to make your negative traits ineffective.

Interesting Asides

The word personality is derived from the word persona, which means "mukhota". There are over 400 values which differentiate a human from an animal.

Graphology is the study of handwriting used to infer a person's character. You will be amused to know that your handwriting and your signature indicate many aspects of your personality and your nature.

I know of a person whose personality changed entirely after his marriage. Before marriage, he was extremely careless, spendthrift, rude, jealous and was never caring for his duties. After marriage, he changed entirely – he became very caring, polite, valued his hard earnings and respectful. Notice and analyse this change in his personality.

Questions to Assess

1) What is worth learning from this lesson?
2) Do your parents emphasize more on your outer appearance or your inner traits?
3) Do you consider addiction to a mobile phone and watching undesired contents, a negative trait?

4) Do your friends love and respect you because of your richness, better dress sense or something else?
5) Whose personality has impressed you the most? Why?
6) Who would you consider as your role model? Try to read his inner personality.

This chapter will help you in becoming soul conscious. You need to take a U-turn and turn from body conscious to soul conscious.

Health is Wealth

If I ask you to choose one out of two – (i) A wealthy individual, possessing all amenities but experiencing poor health, grappling with issues of indigestion, and facing sleep deprivation. Or (ii) a simple person with less riches but enjoying good health. I know that most of you will go with the second option. You will choose the one who is eating properly and gets a sound sleep because **Health is the biggest wealth.** If we ask a rich person about the reasons for his ill health, he may answer that during his childhood, he used to be fond of junk/street food and he ignored the advice of his elders to have a balanced diet. He always avoided eating the food given by his mother and was fond of only oily and fast food like samosas, cold drinks, pizzas, burgers etc. during his childhood. When anyone used to tell him the harmful effects of junk food, he used to laugh at those people. He used to be proud in saying that he could even digest stones. In his youth, he frequently travelled for business, often skipping breakfast, settling for working lunches, consuming excessive tea during meetings with business partners, and neglecting his health. He reassured everyone that he would eventually abandon junk food, break free from unhealthy habits, transition to satvik food, and prioritize his health as he aged. However, by the time he reached that stage, altering his habits proved to be a challenging endeavour.

Here, I will like to share about a research done by a university. If one attains the age of 60 and wants to change any of his habits, it usually takes 60 months to change. For a 50 year old person, this time may be 30 months; for a 40 year old, it may take 15 months but for a 14 years old child, only 21 days are sufficient to change a habit. Therefore it's always recommended to start early, drive slowly and reach safely. Now is the time for you to start, if you do not want to suffer at a later stage. It may be painful for a few days but then you will enjoy good health for the rest of your life and you will possess wealth of both kinds - wealth that everyone craves for and wealth in terms of health too.

Out of all the organs, the tongue is the most powerful one. Although it looks very simple and soft, it is really very difficult to control it. If you control your tongue, you will get control over your power of speech and power of taste too. Speech is important for maintaining good relations but is indirectly responsible for our mental health. A healthy sense of taste is good for our physical health. Tongue has a direct connection with your health because it is the entry point of intake of all your food. It is the tongue that makes you addicted to junk/fast food. You will have to repent of such eating habits (of your adolescence and youth), in your old age. Now the question arises - what to do to avoid these habits. Awake now and take wise steps to take care of your health. Merely going to the gym and spending money is not the solution. Some universal principles need to be adopted. Prevention is always better than cure. This is your habit formation stage and you should not postpone the plan of healthy living. You should proceed gradually and slowly. You must know the role of carbohydrates, fats, vitamins and minerals in your daily life style.

Merely absence of a disease is not the sign of any healthy living. There are certain systems and we should know these systems well. Yes, it's true that you need calories to carry out your day to day tasks. Every food has a specific amount of calories in it. For normal functioning of your body, you require 1440K calories daily. If your work is mechanical in nature and you require a lot of physical strength for carrying it out, then you can definitely seek more calories. But this body is having a limited capacity and excess of everything is bad. So you must put a ceiling on every kind of intake. You should be choosy in selecting the food, not with a view point of taste, but keeping your health in mind. Just keep a check on how fibrous is your food, how easily it will get digested and how much energy will it provide? Your food should not lead to constipation. The habit of proper eating should be developed from the very beginning. Later on, even if you will stop taking junk or fatty food, you will feel as if you are doing a sacrifice or as if there is no charm left in your life. Instead, it should be a natural process.

Develop the habit of taking 4 to 5 glasses of lukewarm water early in the morning. It is advisable to keep an electric bottle near your bed so as to avoid disturbing others. You must drink water as soon as you wake up. This will help you in always feeling fresh. Develop the habit of getting up early in the morning. You'll feel fresh and inhale a lot of oxygen. When you breathe in the open, you inhale more oxygen because there is more scope of photosynthesis in the plants during early hours of the morning. That is why many elderly people remain healthy throughout their lives. This nascent oxygen oxidises all the viral infection which you acquire from polluted air throughout the day. Viral infection takes time to make space inside your bodies but if they get oxidised then they are no longer harmful. You must go for a jog and spend about 30 minutes on it. This is the best insurance you can provide to yourself. Instead of reading late at night, try the same in early morning. Your physical as well as mental health will be fine. After getting fresh and taking a proper bath, get ready for breakfast. Instead of having stuffed *paranthas*, try oats and drink milk. It is always recommended to have some gap between taking milk and the rest of the food. If you can't manage the time, it's fine. But do not miss breakfast.

Mix some nutritional supplements with milk. Eat *Chyavanprash* in winters. It is better to make a routine to take 5 almonds per day. Soak the almonds overnight, peel the skin in the morning and then consume. If you have the temptation for junk food, you should not take it at lunch or dinner. You may take it during breakfast, because it takes more time to digest. Usually after lunch and dinner, people eat fruits. This should be avoided. You should eat fruits first and rest of the food stuff i.e. chapati, vegetables, salad etc. after the fruits. The reason for this is that it's easier to digest the fruits than to digest the other food items. Therefore, if the fruits are eaten earlier, they will not cause the acidity otherwise it generally upsets the stomach. Diet should be balanced. It should contain all nutrients that are required for your growth. You should also avoid drinking water immediately after the food because it obstructs in digesting the food. Do not drink cold water. The fire (jatharagni) created by the body gets low and creates problems in digestion. In the present days, you prefer eating outside meals, just to avoid the cooking. To make the preparation tastier, they add Ajinomoto which is harmful for the health. You should eat to live and not live to eat. During your adolescent age, the liver and other body parts are responsible for digestion but as you grow, your body revolts. It is better to mend the habit at an early age only and you should not compel your parents to have outside food unless there's some emergency. You should avoid eating non vegetarian food at least till you are a student, because non vegetarian food creates anxiety and fear in you which are harmful for your mental health.

A large variety is available in vegetarian diets to provide us with the same energy as a non-vegetarian diet. If you really want to enjoy your food, it is better to be quiet while eating and your full attention should be towards the food only. While eating the food, focus on the palate. Enjoy each morsel that is being put in the mouth. Avoid hurry and curry. Do not sit in front of the TV while eating food, because you will also eat the contents being relayed on the TV along with the food. Be calm and quiet and don't eat when you are angry. You should avoid overeating, rather consume less than your appetite. People are not ill because of eating less but they generally fall ill because of overeating.

Coming to the mental health, the most important observation is that your physical health is directly proportional to your mental health. When you are angry, sad, or frustrated, the chemicals released by the body are toxic and are responsible for indigestion. Indigestion leads to constipation and constipation is the root cause of many other problems like headache, blood pressure etc. Insecurity, jealousy and tensions lead to fatal diseases like cancer. If the mind is tension free, your immune system gets stronger. If any virus from air or water attacks you, your own system will fight with it. To keep your mind free, the best course is to live in the present because the past is past and the future is uncertain. So we must live in the present moment.

This is the reason that "present" is called a present (gift). Laughter is the best medicine. If there are not many chances of natural laughter, you can manage with the artificial laughter too. If any problem comes, take it as a challenge, cope with the problem and keep your routine unchanged. You should control what is in your hands and communicate or share with someone whom you trust. If no one is there to listen, then share with GOD. Join some sports academy. It will help you mentally as well as physically. If joining an academy is not possible, then you can make a group of friends, but take care that your company is good. Read good books and avoid bad company. If possible, take at least one meal with all the members of the family, in a day. Chit chat before or after the meal can help in relaxing. You should have enough courage to admit your faults in front of others and you should be ready to face the consequences. These habits will keep you in maintaining a sound mental health. When you hide anything, the fear of getting exposed will disturb you mentally. You will find that this will affect your appetite too. It's better to fast if your mood is off.

Now-a-days, we are facing another bigger challenge of adulteration. People have become so selfish that for their petty gains, they don't even mind injecting some chemicals to get better and fast ripening fruits. Many banned fertilizers and chemicals are used to yield a better crop. In our country, these are used 300% more than in other countries. Illiteracy and ignorance is also a cause for the same. For their selfish purpose, businessmen usually advise and sell the pesticides much more than the recommended quantity to the farmers. The farmers use pesticides much more than the required quantity. Even colouring and waxing of fruits is done. The cows eat grass and food that is adulterated with urea, and therefore gives adulterated and urea filled milk which is harmful for your health. If you can manage some space in your home, it's better to have your own kitchen garden. Using the simple cow dung manure, you can get enough vegetables for your own consumption. Of course, this will be little costly, but you will have the satisfaction that you are not getting adulterated vegetables. You should always be alert while buying food from the market. You must prefer the seasonal fruits only as other fruits are procured from the cold storage which is costly and not worthy. GOD has planned fruits and food as per your need but not as per your greed. God gives you signals and warnings whenever you disobey the laws of health. But you just compensate for this loss by taking some medicines. Medicines cure one disease and lays the foundation for the other one. Why don't you listen to the voice of God who is prompting you from inside (and even outside) in the form of different types of ill effects caused to your body by consuming such a food? Now-a-days, some of the children of your age are also suffering from the problem of being diabetic.

Nip the evil in the bud. Whenever you feel that you are not obeying the laws of health, you should immediately promise yourself not to go in the direction that will ruin your old age. Healthy mind resides in a healthy body. Both are complementary to each other. Take care of your mental health by being positive and this will improve your physical health also.

Assets :
Inquisitive Questions
1) Why is laughter the best and the sweetest medicine for both mind and body?
2) Why is it so difficult to lose belly fat in adults?
3) You want to eat a lot. How do you force yourself to eat less in this condition?

4) "Laughter boosts the immune system". Do you agree with this? Give reasons.
5) Does happiness make you healthy and wealthy? How?
6) How does physical and mental health depend on the financial condition of a person?
7) How to take care of mental health?

Interesting Asides

1) A country has started a new ticket vending machine at one of their metro stations... "30 squats and get a ticket". It's not about money but it shows:- How careful the government is about the health of people !!!!
2) Even if you laugh artificially, the positivity for health will be the same because your subconscious mind cannot distinguish between natural and artificial laughter.
3) For a normal person, 1440 calories per day is required, but we usually take over 5000 calories.
4) In less than a minute, your heart can pump blood to every cell in your body. And over the course of a day, about 100,000 heartbeats shuttle 2,000 gallons of oxygen rich blood, through about 60,000 miles (2.5 Circles around earth) of branching blood vessels that link together the cells of our organs and body parts. That's a hefty job for a fist-sized muscle. The heart beats around 3 billion times in the average person's life.

Suggestive Activity

There are many celebrities and common persons who have reduced their weight and lost fat substantially. Meet any one such person and share their fat-to-fit journey.

Make a habit to read a funny book or watch a comedy show. This will make laughter and humour a priority for you. Practice laughter yoga. Share laughter with friends.

Day to Day Relevance
1) Health is the biggest wealth in life. If you keep yourself healthy, you will automatically get the desired happiness and enjoyment. There are many people who do not have good wealth, but you will find them happy and satisfied. They have love in their life and enjoy good health. On the other hand, people who are having tons of money, live in a state of fear and depression. It is important to pay attention to your health more than your money.
2) Physical health is affected by mental health. So take care of mental health also.
3) Your only duty is to be happy- Swami Ramatirath.

Value Content
> We should not waste our energy by overusing our senses.
> Our body is a limited company.

Questions to Assess
1) You must have read about people who are on hunger strike or some saints who are on fast for days together. What will happen if you don't eat but just take water for 15 days?
2) Is laughter contagious?
3) How does your mental condition affect your physical health? How do your anger, sadness, tensions and frustration affect your body?
4) What is the best diet plan to lose weight and to keep yourself fit?
5) What will happen to your body if you don't change your eating habits but you do the workout daily?
6) Suggest a suitable diet to maintain mental health.

Day 20
Unity in Diversity

Diversity is an inherent characteristic in all walks of life. It is evident in the smallest of things. For instance, a simple thumb impression is the basis of our unique identification in this vast plethora of humans. Our different interests give rise to an array of various talents in a number of fields – be it science or mathematics or arts. One can stand out for having different tastes from his own siblings despite having the same background and the same upbringing.

Why is this Diversity so important? Imagine a world of clones – where everyone looks identical, thinks the same and performs the same set of chores every day. It will be like watching a movie with only one protagonist. Life will be a smooth ride without any emotions associated with it. There will neither be any joy at achieving a goal nor any drive to do better when falling short. Just imagine the game of *tambola*, if all of us get the same tickets (with the same places), will there be any charm? Will there be any enthusiasm in the game? Everyone will finish the game at the same time. Imagine a rainbow in the sky with just one color. How will it look? It is the diversity of colours which adds glamour to the rainbow. Similarly, a lot of different flowers make a beautiful bouquet. To sum up, the entire world would cease to exist, if there is no diversity. At this point, we can take a second to thank the Almighty; because HE in HIS infinite wisdom has perpetuated these tiny differences between us, which give the true flavour to our everyday lives.

This just highlights our futility in getting annoyed with someone for simply not adhering to our definition of acceptable behaviour. If we simply remember that a person's reaction is pursuant of his/her basic nature, we would not get angry at all. Instead of trying to change others, it is much easier to teach ourselves to accept our colleagues and acquaintances as they are. Strength lies in differences, not in similarities. GOD has created us to celebrate these differences. Negative feelings like jealousy and antipathy should have no place in our hearts and minds. One should not feel jealous of the possessions of others. Diversity is not about how we differ, but it is about embracing one another's uniqueness. Rather one should accept GOD as a director who gives difficult roles to the best actor. The best player is the one who concentrates on his cards and uses the right card at the right time, without bothering about what his/her rivals have got. Let us have no ill feelings against others. Enjoy the diversity. Someone may be ahead of you in one field or the other. You should not compete with others; instead, your competition should be with your own self.

Sri Sathya Sai baba quotes "Love All, Serve All, Help Ever and Hurt Never". This principle, if we try and emulate it in our lives, will culminate in having healthy relations with others and also with self and GOD. For leading a happy, contented and successful life, it is imperative to realize and introspect about our shortcomings and strive hard to improve upon them. The most important thing is to have peace in our inner self. Peace can only be achieved if we enjoy the diversity of nature. See the sky at night. There are many stars; each one is unique in itself. All of them are making the sky so beautiful. Go to the garden. Just see how beautiful each flower is. Appreciate the beauty of nature; offer your gratitude to the Almighty GOD for giving such a beautiful earth to live in. You will feel peace within yourself. Peace will, in turn, give you energy to work. The same energy, if utilized to compare your possessions with others, to feel jealous and to curse GOD (that why has HE not given much to you and why others are enjoying more privilege than you), will hamper your progress. Be thankful to GOD for what HE has given to you and be ready to help the underprivileged. Understand the concept of diversity. Watch the differences in languages, culture, traditions and food of different parts of your country. You must understand that you are the children of "*Bharat Mata*" and enjoy the rich heritage of your country. Accept all colours of life and then plan and paint a beautiful picture. How can we get the music of life without combining seven *sur* (musical notes)? Just imagine the tune with only one note. Can you get pleasure without the variation of beats by a *dholak* master? Do not get afraid of ups and downs in your life. Without the night, how can you enjoy the light of day? Without pain, how will you assess the value of pleasure? Find out an opportunity in every situation.

Nothing is by chance. GOD wants you to learn to sail your own boat of life in tide and turbulence. Very soon you will get bored, if you will not find any diversity in life. That is why you will always find someone ahead of you and someone behind you. Do not have EGO if you are ahead, but have empathy with those who are behind you. This world is a stage and all of us play our act. Concentrate on your role, do your duty and do it with perfection. This should be your aim. Let us welcome the diversity and enlarge our vision.

There is another reason for you to welcome the diversity of language, caste, culture, religion, color etc. There are chances that you lose your patience and develop anger if you do not welcome and enjoy the diversity. As already discussed, anger takes away the intelligence and your peace of mind is lost. This does not mean that you should not love your individuality but you should also have respect for others too. When you enjoy the diversity, you will have peace of mind. Most of the time, you keep fighting because of the difference of opinions or the difference of taste. You lose your peace of mind when your opponents don't like what you like. Almost 90% of your problems exist, because you do not welcome the diversity and you want to change the opponent as per your liking and your viewpoint. This is also the reason for the existence of issues between you and your parents because you want them to welcome whatever you like and they expect the same from you. With the passage of time, your relationship with your parents becomes tense and the charm of life goes away, because you have to live with them. It is a two way process and is applicable to you as well as to your parents, but it is tilted little towards them because of the experiences of life which they possess and you do not.

Another advantage of enjoying the diversity is preserving your energy that otherwise, gets wasted in making others convince and agree to your opinions or views. They may agree to you momentarily in your presence but may not be with your opinions forever. Their nature will prompt them to go as per their own likings and this is going to be the source of anger and frustration in you. This wastage of energy will hamper your progress. Better you love the creation of GOD and do not try to change others. Let us imagine that you are going on your scooter and some obstacle, like a big stone or a pit hole comes your way, won't you change your path? You will surely change the course. So it is advisable to enjoy everything that GOD has given to you. Be thankful to HIM and develop patience towards others. LIVE AND LET LIVE.

See the UNITY IN DIVERSITY in nature with so many languages, religions and cultures. In spite of these diversities, we are all Indians. Though all the stars are unique, when combined, they are called a galaxy (of stars). There is only one language which is the language of the heart. God has given everyone the same human body containing two eyes, two ears, one nose, two hands, two feet and most importantly the same soul. The world of music is soothing to your ears, because there are seven *sur* (notes). All the *sur* with various permutations and combinations unite to produce a sweet melody.

Assets :
Inquisitive Questions
1) What do you mean by diversity?
2) Name a few diversities which you observe.
3) What are the common differences that we have with our rivals?
4) How the world would be, if there is no diversity?
5) Why are there wars in the world?

6) How can we be happy and peaceful?

7) Define the relation between secularism and diversity?

8) "Your competition is with yourself". Justify this statement.

Suggestive Activity

You enjoy teaching your younger ones and declare that you will be joining the teaching profession. Guess what will be the opinion of your parents, siblings and friends? Had you been in their place, would your reaction differ?

Prepare a chart/depicting food, clothes, languages, weather, tourist places etc. of the different states of India. Observe the diversity and sum up your observations in the form of an article.

Interesting Asides

Just pass the light through the prism, you would see that light would deviate to seven beautiful colours named VIBGYOR. If the same seven colours are passed through an inverted prism, these seven colours unite again to form white light. This is a clear cut example of diversity and from diversity to unity. Nature is full of many such examples.

A Reporter was interviewing an old couple and asked them the secret of their age. The couple replied that they never had an argument. The Reporter said that it was not possible that they never had an argument during their entire married life. The couple replied that the reporter might be right.

Value Content

Let us learn to disagree. Because you are seeing the problem standing on one side and you have not visited the other side of the problem. We must remember that every coin has two sides. We just need to identify the correct side and take the decisions accordingly.

Day to Day Relevance

The family remains well knit if we welcome the opinions of each other. The head of the family assigns the duty as per capability and interests of the individual family members. The same mantra is applicable for any successful organization.

Questions to Assess

1) What will you do when you realize that your rival is trying to provoke you intentionally?
2) Why do we generally observe the differences in a father and son?
3) You are participating in a debate and you feel the audience does not like your idea. What would be your reaction then?
4) Imagine a world without any diversity - the same states, same nature, same age, same culture, same language, same customs, same dresses etc. Write an article on this presumption.

Day 21
Purpose of Life

GOD has given different talents to each individual. In every game, different kinds of talent are required. For example, we need batsmen, bowlers and all-rounders in cricket. Similarly we need different kinds of experts in hockey. Likewise, in the game of life, there is a requirement of every kind of personality. The need is to understand the talent in yourself and plan your life accordingly. Without planning and without setting the purpose of life, it is like a ship sailing in sea without any direction, just roaming with the current of the wind. Till class 8th, generally we are generally unknown about our talent, but now it should be a serious concern to fix the purpose of life. Once the purpose of life is fixed, we can start working in that direction but while choosing the purpose of life, everyone should be very conscious and focussed.

What are the Do's and Don'ts while going in for choosing the goal of our life. The ultimate purpose of life is to help the society with your presence. You have to start early for this. Just check your interest, and then plan on how your interest can help the society. You usually start with "I", then go to "A" and then to "S". It means you first see your personal benefits, then of the Association, i.e. family and friends and then comes the turn of the Society but it should be SAI instead of IAS. While setting the purpose of life, think how you can help the society with your talent and with your unique qualities, without ignoring yourself. If you decide to go for the commerce stream, then you will help the society in banking, accounts, taxation and other related work. If you choose the medical field, naturally you will try to become a doctor and hence serve the society in curing people and getting rid of their health problems. The education which you are getting should be to help the society. Remember "*Propakaram idam Shareeram*". This body is given by GOD to serve others. Do not go for any peer pressure in deciding your career path. Go for the choice of subjects as per your own interest and capabilities, where you feel that you can give your best and prove beneficial to the society. The real purpose of life is to please GOD and His creation. First you should serve your parents who brought you to this world. While keeping the objective of serving our nation, your aim should be to strive hard in that direction to achieve your target. Once you decide your goal, you should start working hard and add all possible efforts that could lead you to achieve the goal. You will find many chances to add information to your goal. Go on adding information for the purpose of transformation.

Purpose of life is to be planned as per the age. Today when you are students, you should obtain all relevant information so that you may apply the same for transformation at a later stage. Unfortunately we get information just for the sake of information only and apply very less in the desired direction. Now as a student, you have fixed your purpose of life which is to serve the nation and the creation of GOD (including yourself). You should also be aware of all the obstacles, which may hinder your goal and should think of the ways to overcome these obstacles. Let us check these one by one. First and the most important obstacle is the company you have around you. Check, if you are keeping the friends who will help you in fulfilling your goal? If not, then try to avoid such companies. Keep a set of friends who are sincere toward their own goals. Check, if you are doing justice with your goal. Are you giving enough time required to serve the purpose? You must know the importance of this human life. You have taken birth on this earth with a special purpose and remember you have to pass the exam of life with flying colours. People should remember you for your good deeds once you leave this world. This is the time when you should 'start early, drive slowly and reach safely' says Sri Sathya Sai Baba. Thirdly, ensure that your goal is not hurting others. Check that your goal/aim should not cause problems to any other positive person (definitely you can hurt the anti-social elements of the society). Priority should be given to the service rather than to the money.

No doubt MNCs pay very good salaries and you intend to join them. But if you are good in academics and have interest in the medical field, then you must go for the same; it may be less paying but chances of serving the society are far more. While choosing your goal, remember that the service to society or GOD's creation is going to frame your destiny. Take required time in choosing your goal but it should not be a wavering goal. Think over the pros and cons of the goal, though you may change it at a later stage, but not advisable. You may or may not get the job or chance to work in a business of your choice, but this should not make you frustrated. Instead of doing whatever you like, you should like whatever you do. But the game of life should be very clear to you. You are the master of your own destiny. Even if hurdles come in, take it as a test from God. God helps those who help themselves. Learn to serve and serve to learn. You have to pay the debt of your parents too. You should not make them sad by your actions. They should be given the priority. If they want to choose a particular goal (or a particular career) for you but you are not interested in it, convince them to do your best. It would be better to go for an aptitude test from some expert counsellor. But then, the result of the outcome should be adhered to.

World is changing very fast. But due to the limited knowledge, you have in your mind only three streams - Arts, Commerce and Science (Medical and Non-Medical). You do not think beyond these. There are many other avenues available now and some of these can be pursued even after completion of 10th class. Better visualise the world after completing your education. You should think of the world on the need based requirement on completion of your education. Just keep in mind about some of the vocational courses too so that if you do not get the job of your choice, then there should be some alternatives available with you. Try to secure a position, where you could have the opportunity to serve the nation. After paying the debt of your parents, you have to pay the dues of your country too. This is the time where you should develop your attitude. Whatever you develop, will give you the results in future accordingly. This is the right time to plan your future. Choose as per your liking and capacity. But be prepared for any situation with a desire to serve the society, because our country has very high expectations from you.

The purpose of life is to lead the life of purpose. Before you leave this world, you should give more than what you have taken from society. Your life should be like a tree which, of course, takes the help of all the 5 elements but gives back many fold. To lead a purposeful life, you must have a very strong foundation. Education is the strong foundation and your sincerity toward studies will give you the chance to serve the society better than anyone else. This world is very cruel and won't support you if you do not stand on your own feet. Respect the time so that time respects you. Remember an old song *"tu na chalega to chal dengi rahein, manzil ko tarsengi teri nigahe"*. "Arise, awake and do not stop till the goal is achieved", says Swami Vivekananda. Once the goal is set, the execution should start. Tell me if you want to draw water from the earth, is it possible if you go on digging the earth at different places. Once you fix one place and go on digging the earth without changing the position, you will get water. Everything in this world happens with a purpose. You are born in this world with a purpose, you are chosen by a purpose.

Here, I have not taken the ultimate purpose of life, thinking it is beyond your scope, at present. Ultimate purpose of your life is to be pure, loving, selfless and impartial like God. Every effort of your working towards the purpose of life, you have chosen, will either lead towards God or will be led away from God. All depends upon your mind set and your efforts in the direction of achieving your goal. If you are doing your duty with the best of your efforts and are constantly aware of your purpose in life, it is sure that you are leading towards the ultimate goal. If you salute your goal, you need not to salute anyone else, even God. But if you pollute your goal, maybe because of your five senses or because of bowing before the insolent minds, you will have to salute every one. Fix your goal, understand the purpose of life and act accordingly or be ready to face the consequences, like a directionless boat faces in a sea. Choice is yours.

Assets :

Inquisitive Questions

1) What do you want to be?
2) Is there any conflict between you or your parents about the choice you are going to make about your goal?
3) What is going to happen if you don't decide about your goal?
4) Do you think that this life is given to you to eat, sleep and be messy only?
5) Do you think that the world is changing so fast and it is impossible to think about your purpose of life?

Interesting Asides

- **Propakaram Idam Shareeram**
  Few Examples of the persons living their life for others:
- **Sindhutai Sapkal** :- Popularly known as "Mother of Orphans", emerged stronger with every difficulty she faced and is a "mother" to over 1400 orphans and children who were abandoned by their parents.
- **Omkarnath Sharma** :- Popularly known as "Medicine Baba", walks around the streets of Delhi, knocking on the doors of relatively well to do households to collect free medicines for the needy.
- **Nandlal Master** :- Has been on a mission to empower women and abolish child labour.
- **Darialli Ramaiah** :- The man who planted more than 10 million trees by selling his three acre plot of land to gather the necessary funds to purchase seeds and plant saplings.

Suggestive Activity

Ask the purpose of life from 10 friends of your class and rank them as per your own vision. Is there anyone in the class who has the same purpose of life as yours?

Day to Day Relevance

When you will read the autobiographies of successful persons, you will find one thing common in all, i.e. that all were aware of their purpose of life. This proves that if you want to be successful, the first requirement is to think and decide about the purpose of life.

Value Content

"The mystery of human existence lies not in just staying alive, but in finding something to live for."

"If you want to be happy, set a goal that commands your thoughts, liberates your energy and inspires your hopes."

Questions to Assess

1) Why is the purpose of life so important?
2) What is the ultimate purpose of life?
3) Elaborate "*Propakaram idam Shareeram*".
4) Why should we not change the purpose of life, once fixed?

Day 22
SWOT Analysis

Today we will discuss the concept of SWOT analysis. You are given human birth and it is your duty to lead a purposeful life. Do you have any plans for your future? Have you planned what you would like to be?

It is very important for us to check it with our SWOT. First letter, **'S'** represents **Strength**. Each one of us has some talent called strength - sometimes we are aware of it and sometimes we are not. Even Lord Hanuman was not aware of His strength, when He went in search of Sita. He was told that to find Sita, He would have to cross the ocean and He was not sure if He would be able to manage it or not. But then his mentors reminded Him of His strength. Likewise, many children do not know their full potential. Some of you may be good in sports, some in a particular subject, some in drawing, some in project making and some in writing stories. But it is certain that you all have a particular area where you are stronger in comparison to other areas. There's a need to know yourself and find out the area of your strength. After recognizing your own capabilities, it's important to demonstrate them to your parents and contemplate how to leverage them in determining your life's purpose. How can you help society using your strengths? Every attempt should be made to know the real potential in you. Your parents must be aware of your strength, because they have watched you growing since your infancy and they know the best in you. Still it is very important to know as to how you use your strengths in your day to day life.

Next comes the second letter **'W'** that denotes your **Weakness**. Without knowing your own weaknesses, you can't get rid of the same. Some of the common weaknesses are negative thinking, fear and procrastination. While locating your weaknesses, your mind should be rational. Your critics are your best friends. After locating the weakness, you should not think that it is not possible to get rid of them. Every problem has a solution and you must be ready to get rid of your weaknesses. First and the most important requisite is the will to improve. If we keep loving your weaknesses, then there's no scope of improvement. Once your vulnerabilities are recognized by others as weaknesses, it's imperative to make an effort to overcome them. As you mature, it becomes a habit to address these weaknesses. Taking action now, fuelled by strong determination, discipline, and prayer, enables you to eliminate these weaknesses. The true purpose of life is to transcend these shortcomings. By the end of your life's journey, you should emerge refined and strengthened.

3rd letter of SWOT is '**O**', that stands for **Opportunities** available to you. First and the most important point is that God has given us the human body and that we are gifted with a super conscious mind to discriminate between right and wrong. We are given 24 hours per day like others. Human life itself is a big opportunity. Basically, every problem and every failure is an opportunity. What is required is to master your mind and be a mastermind. As you think so you are; dust you think dust you are and GOD you think God you are. There are enormous examples in the history of mankind, where people have accomplished impossible tasks with their strong determination. World is full of opportunities but only the attitude required to make use of them. Winner never quits and the quitter never wins. One must read the autobiography of our ex-President, APJ Abdul Kalam. With a meagre source of income, he could reach the post of President. Even Our PM Modi Ji is no exception. There is no limit to opportunities. You are blessed with parents who are always willing to help you out. You can use your *Viveka* (intellect) and set the things right. You are given enough guidance to achieve your aim.
You have to make the most of every Opportunity. Let me tell you a small story:

A wealthy man with four sons devises a test to determine who will inherit his fortune based on who values his hard-earned wealth the most. He gives each son five grains of rice and informs them that he will inquire about the grains in five years, awarding his property to the son who demonstrates the greatest appreciation for them. After five years, the first son discards the grains, the second son consumes them, and the third son preserves them in a silver box, offering prayers for their safety. Meanwhile, the fourth son plants the grains, cultivating them into a bountiful rice crop over the years, resulting in a vast land filled with rice fields by the end of the five-year period.

Who do you think will get the father's property after 5 years? Obviously, the father gave his property to his fourth son, as he was the most deserving amongst his four sons. So, whenever you have anything little with you, look at opportunities to grow it.

Last but not the least is the 4th letter "**T**", which stands for **Threat**. When you miss the opportunities, you will start getting threats. Suppose you are preparing for your exam, you have ample opportunity to go for the preparation by investing a few hours from already 24 hours given by GOD. But if you do not avail the opportunities, then threat comes into play. Threat of getting failed or scoring low marks, start knocking at your door. Procrastination is another threat. Negative thinking, poor will power, fear of criticism and six vices are also the threats for your growth. Check which of the threats is more prominent in you. Deal firmly with your threats and nurture your strengths. Get rid of your weaknesses. Threat is nothing but a general kind of weakness, which GOD has created for you to test your growth.

Assets :
Inquisitive Questions
1) Have you ever done a SWOT analysis on yourself? Do it today. Try it for a week.
2) Does SWOT really work for you?

3) An Opportunity for one can be a Threat for another. How do you explain this?
4) How would you define the SWOT for a Science and a Commerce student?
5) Can you think of any disadvantages of SWOT analysis?
6) "Winner never quits and quitter never wins". Explain.

Interesting Asides

If we do the SWOT analysis of our country, we notice that we have the maximum percentage of youth ready to work for the country. This is our STRENGTH. Our WEAKNESS is the selfishness of political leaders. Our illiteracy and blind faith to discriminate between right and wrong is another biggest WEAKNESS of our country. OPPORTUNITY is that Indians are very good at computers and programming. We can earn much more revenue for our country by providing intellectual services to the western countries. Our THREAT is unemployment and our youth preferring for white collar jobs only.

It is up to you to consider a given situation as an Opportunity or as a Problem. In the same situation, one can find immense opportunity, whereas another person can run away from it by posing it as a problem. There goes a small story to illustrate this:
Many years ago two salesmen were sent by a shoe company to Africa to find out if there was a market for shoes. The first salesman reported back, "There is no market there - nobody wears shoes." The second salesman reported back, "There is a huge market - nobody wears shoes." You can look at the same situation in two different ways - negatively or positively. The first salesman looked at it as a Problem; the second one looked at it as an Opportunity.

Suggested Activity

1) D.C. Model Group of Schools is planning to open another branch in Mohali. The management has already acquired the land and has

sufficient funds to start the new School in Mohali. You are required to visit the proposed site, have meetings with the management and conduct a thorough SWOT Analysis for opening a new school branch. Describe the feasibility and growth prospects of the proposed new branch.

2) Prepare a list of your strengths and weaknesses.

Day to Day Relevance

1) SWOT analysis is a useful methodology to evaluate and formulate the strategy for an organization or a business. A deeper analysis of SWOT will help in business establishment and growth. These should focus on :

Strengths – Advantages, Knowledge, Experience, Resources, Location, Capabilities, Reliability, Reputation etc.

Weaknesses – Disadvantages, Lack of experience, Poor financial backup, Location, Lack of key staff etc.

Opportunities – Partnerships, New product development, Import/ Export, Technology, Innovation etc.

Threats – Loss of partners, Competition, Inflation, Price-war, Manpower turnover etc.

2) Frank and sincere SWOT analysis by any individual has the potential to revolutionize

Value Content

SWOT Analysis is a powerful tool to understand your Strengths and Weaknesses and to identify the Opportunities and the Threats you face as a student and afterwards.

Core qualities are your Strengths – like Self Confidence, Honesty, Punctuality.

Pitfalls are your Weaknesses – like Arrogance, Lack of confidence, Physical or Mental state.

New challenges are Opportunities – like Competition, Examination. **Allergies that you find difficult to handle are the Threats** – like Submissive nature, Posting in a remote area.

Questions to Assess

1) How do you do the SWOT analysis of yourself?
2) Do you consider SWOT analysis really useful or do you consider it a wasteful exercise? Give reasons.
3) What would be a good SWOT analysis of our Prime Minister, of your class teacher and of your parents?
4) What are some of the strong and weak points of work environment in a
    - BPO
    - IT company
    - School
    - Manufacturing Plant
    - Hotel/Restaurant
5) Create an example where Opportunity for one is Threat for the other.

Law of Karma

Have you ever pondered why your friend is wealthier than you are? Or why one student seems to evade detection while cheating, whereas you were caught the first time you attempted it? Why do you score fewer marks in spite of studying so hard, while your friend, who rarely studies, scores well? Why are you and your family going through tough times when you never did anything wrong to anyone? Why do you have to suffer because of other's acts? In this *Kalyuga*, when the dishonest enjoys and the honest suffers, why should you remain honest? What is the sin of an innocent new-born who is born with a disability? And if everything is already written in your destiny, then why should you work hard and remain true to your principles? The answer to all these questions is not simple for other religions but for our sanatan dharma it is not tough as we believe in rebirth and as per our ideology this life of ours is part of the journey which we are going through for millions of years.

Dear children, these are a few common questions which disturb all of us and we don't find their answers easily. There are many more such questions. No one is sure about the logic and most of us are still searching for the answers. Still, I would like to answer these questions and justify the same with the help of "**Law of Karma**". This law of karma is a unique discovery of ancient India. To understand the game of life and the law of karma, we have to assume something as we do in Algebra, while solving equations. Have you ever pondered why our organs cease to function upon death, despite everything else in our body remaining intact? Certainly there is something unknown which leaves our body when we die. Let us assume it to be the subtle body (*suksham shareer*). Let us now discuss the contents of this subtle body. Actually, it contains prints/impressions of all our actions, memories, learning and deeds. When we take rebirth, this subtle body enters a new body. But let us understand the role played by this subtle body in choosing a prospective mother. You will always be assessed as per your karma. Extent of *punya/paap* (virtue/sin) earned in your previous birth will decide the merit of your subtle body. While choosing a mother (to take birth on this earth), you will be assessed as per your accumulated karma and right of selection will be taken by another claimant with higher merit for the same mother.

In the beginning (when we start our life), we get a colourless subtle body. Rubrics are set for each and every Karma that we are indulged in. Our subtle body gets a colour; black or white as per our karmas. White is the result of good karmas and black is the result of bad karmas. With the combination of so many karmas, we get a final colour at the end of life. It can be greyish black or greyish white, depending upon the quality of work done by us. There can be crores of shades possible because with every one addition of black or white, the shade changes. This process of rewarding and punishing is continuous and comprehensive. Throughout the life, it is in auto mode. There is no partiality, no favour and no error. It is a fool proof system attached to everyone irrespective of caste, colour and creed. Since this process is designed by GOD, it is universal and applicable to the entire world. If we tease our classmates for amusement, it means that we are adding black to our subtle body and if we help someone without any expectation, we add white to our subtle body. There are enough pieces of evidence to prove it and from time to time, GOD sends a divine person to teach us the forgotten lessons. To make the game interesting, HE has planned that there is no communication between the world of the subtle bodies and our world. Still, some rare shreds of evidence are available and it appears that the world after death is very pleasant and better than our earth, if our karmas are good. Otherwise, our ancient literature tells us that there are two kinds of world, normally called Hell and Heaven.

Let us understand the nature of the world of subtle bodies. Here, I would like to mention that there is a degree of variation in hell and heaven. There are seven worlds and each world has 9 stages which imply that there are 63 (7X9) milestones. The lower three worlds i.e. 1, 2, 3 are like hell, the world 4 is like our world and the upper three worlds i.e. 5,6,7 are like heaven. The person who belongs to world one and stage one is highly immoral and has not done anything good at all. His subtle body will be completely black. He is a sufferer and gets rigorous punishment in the world of the subtle bodies. These people are selfish and throughout life exploit others for their selfish gains .When they finish their journey of life here and go to a new world they are being punished for their wrong deeds. Even when they come back to earth their past deeds force them to compromise and usually they are deprived of some advantage which the others enjoy because of their deeds of past life. The progress from one stage to the next stage is very slow in the mortal world. If someone is in a hurry to jump to the next stage, the only solution is to come to the earth by taking rebirth, face the punishment and get rid of the black as much as possible. Eliminating bad karma may be achievable through the presence of certain handicaps that individuals may have from early childhood. This addresses the question of why a child may be born blind, deaf, or with any physical disadvantage, under the assumption that since the child has not wronged anyone (if we view it as a fresh start).

Now I can easily respond to the previous questions. A child is born blind not because of the karma of this life. He, being blind, had selected the option to take birth and come back to the earth to pay for his karmas. You might feel that righteous people suffer more on the earth. In fact, they are not suffering; rather they are only getting rid of their bad karmas here. It was their choice, when they come to this world which they have forgotten. If you've borrowed money from a bank and the bank manager happens to be your friend, what recommendation might the bank manager offer? He will always advise you to pay back the instalments of the bank in time so that you may become a good customer and the bank may enhance your credit limit. Similar are the ways of GOD. HE wishes that since it is less time consuming and easy to get rid of the bad deeds on earth, it is better to pay the debt and enjoy life after death. So do good deeds and keep adding whites to your subtle body and improve your merit. Once you improve, you will enjoy life at both the places; here on the earth as well as in the world of mortals.

When observing a person who has consistently been dishonest and seemingly found pleasure in it, one might question how they will recognize their wrongdoing. The analogy drawn here is akin to a good teacher ensuring that students understand their mistakes in exams and the reasons for marks being deducted. Similarly, it is believed that after the "exam" of life concludes, God offers individuals a platform to comprehend the ramifications of their actions. This suggests that there should be a life after death where one can witness the results of their earthly deeds, providing an opportunity for reflection and understanding. While residing in the mortal world, it's evident that ill-gotten wealth can wreak havoc on the lives of future generations. Court battles and conflicts plague the family, causing suffering for the dishonest individual's children and grandchildren. Conversely, those who lead an honest life on Earth find solace and inner peace, even in the realm of subtle existence, as they witness their family thriving and flourishing.

When we plan to take rebirth, there are two options with us. The first option is to go into an environment where everything is in scarcity and we get the punishment to get rid of our bad karmas easily and then return with a higher position. The second option is to choose a place of comfort, do good deeds and improve upon the merits. We decide it ourselves but the tragedy is that when we take rebirth, we forget everything of our planning. The luxuries and privileges we experience are the result of our good deeds in action. Just as a fixed deposit in a bank multiplies, restraining our desires and leading a simple life means using fewer "white" (good karma) for yourself, thereby increasing the likelihood of improvement.

GOD will give you a promotion in the world of subtle bodies too. If you use your money for charitable purposes, help others and do not hurt others, you are preparing the ground for a better position after death. Love all, serve all and do not miss the opportunity to serve others as this is the only way to progress. Ultimately you have to reach to the 7th stage and finally to a stage where GOD receives you. Whenever your friends get any undue privilege, do not feel jealous of them, rather understand that it is because of their previous karmas that help them. Using white means you are using earnings of your good karma to satisfy your sensory pleasure or EGO. Suppose you have donated one lakh rupees to an institution, got it published and got recognition from the society, this means that you are using white. Using black means that you have taken the punishment of your bad karma or GOD has given you the punishment in terms of disease, insult, financial loss etc. When you go through the sufferings, bear patiently thinking that your karma (black) is paid. Usually everyone wants to postpone the use of black but ready to use the white to satisfy one's EGO. It is better to use it to the minimum so that you may save it to get a good position in the world of subtle bodies.

Now, you may think that if everything is predestined, then what is the use of doing any labour or hard work? GOD has given you a free will to improve your merit. As per Indian mythology we cannot compensate for a bad deed by doing a good one. Accounts of karma differ from the banking system where positives compensate for negatives and vice versa. We need to be careful as we cannot compensate for the loss. Today you are bullying your friend and tomorrow you give him a treat and you think you have now paid back the negative. You will be rewarded or punished for your good and bad deeds respectively.

 The black that you have added cannot be cancelled by white, but by adding more white you can improve the shade and hence the merit. Man is the maker of his own destiny. You cannot blame GOD for your sufferings. If you want to enjoy your life, the game is to make someone happy. The choice is yours.

Let me clarify this with an example of the law of karma. Suppose you go to a coffee shop where you pay for your coffee at the counter and have your cup from the counter itself. Now when you reach the counter, you see a person getting Rs. 85 and you feel surprised that you are paying Rs. 15 from your pocket and the other one is getting the money. Here the problem is that you have not observed the full scene. You have not seen the person paying a hundred rupee note to the person at the counter. Likewise, if someone enjoys the benefit without making any effort in comparison to your efforts, remember it may be due to its past payment. Man is the maker of his own destiny. You do not know your past, because past is past and future is the outcome of present. This is the reason we call presents a present (gift). So live in the present and do good deeds to make your destiny better. Good karma is like a wallet in your pocket. Use them judiciously so that you may not have a shortage of funds. Remember you have to become warrior and not worrier (who have sleepless nights with a fear of punishment because of their bad deeds).

Assets:
Inquisitive Questions:
1. Do you believe that all major events in our life are pre-destined? Elaborate.
2. Can you relate Karma and the Law of "Give-and-Take"
3. Are major disasters destined?
4. Is "Karma" something to do with "Fate"? Explain.
5. Does the Karma of present life affect our destiny? Explain.

Interesting Asides
A child asked GOD: If everything is already written in destiny, then why should I wish?

God smiled and said: Maybe on some pages, I have written, "As you wish".

Suggestive Activity

Let us prepare a merit solution. Assume the white color as good karma and black color as the bad karma. Now take a glass of water and add a few drops of black color. Now, add double the drops of white in this. Alternatively, let us do the vice versa. In the glass of pure water, add a few drops of white and double the black color. You observe which one is the light grey and which one is the dark grey.

Now ask yourself, who is more meritorious and why? You get the next birth as per the merits you have gained. Now speak a few lines on "Man is the maker of his own destiny".

Day to Day Relevance

1. We believe that our life is moving as per our Karmas of the past. Similarly our life in the next birth will be as per our Karmas in the present. So keep on doing your best, acquiring Merits and avoiding Sins.

2. If we consider GOD as impartial, then why a person is born blind, why one gets placed in a rich family and one in a poor family in a slum area. Born in the same family with equal opportunities, one gets the job of a Manager who sits in an AC room and another one gets a job in a factory working under peak summer and peak winters. All these prove that we get birth, wealth, family and opportunities as per our old deeds i.e. Karmas.

Value Content

Your every selfless positive deed will generate "merit" and your every negative deed will generate "demerit". This is as per the "Karmas".

It is a good saying that **"How people treat you is their Karma; how you react is yours"**. So react carefully.

Questions to Assess

1. There is a saying "As you sow, so shall you reap". How do you relate this saying to the Theory of Karma?
2. What is the true purpose of life? Is it to overcome Karma?
3. Can meditation change your karmas?
4. It is said that we will merge with GOD when our subtle body will be colourless, meaning no black and no white. How can this stage be possible?
5. How will you convince yourself to lead a simple life and earn whites for the next inning?

Indeed, there's a concerning trend of increasing commercialization in society. In the past, we cherished relationships and valued people over material possessions. However, today, there's a shift where we prioritize things over individuals, leading to a rise in selfish behaviour. People readily accept favours and assistance from others but often fail to express gratitude or reciprocate when the opportunity arises. This imbalance in expectations can strain relationships and breed negative sentiments.

It's crucial to acknowledge the importance of expressing gratitude. When someone extends kindness or support, it's only fair to show appreciation through simple words. This gesture doesn't require any monetary investment but holds immense value in strengthening bonds and fostering goodwill.

Let us understand - what restrains people from offering gratitude. Some time ago, we invited a group of Kashmiri students to visit our home. We dedicated considerable time, effort, and resources to ensure they received VIP treatment and were pleased with their experience. However, upon their departure, they failed to express gratitude. It dawned on me that they perceived our hospitality as their entitlement, perhaps even viewing their visit as a favour to us. The absence of a simple "Thank you very much for your hospitality" sentence caused our relationship to sour. Occasionally, individuals tend to perceive certain privileges as their entitlement without acknowledging the efforts and time invested by others. Instead of expressing gratitude, they may adopt an overly confident attitude, casually mentioning their own backup plans. This behaviour could stem from ego, as they fear that expressing thanks might diminish their perceived position and dignity. A nice quote by William Arthur Ward says: "**Feeling gratitude and not expressing it, is like wrapping a present and not giving it.**"

The mentality regarding gratitude can sometimes be influenced by parental attitudes. For instance, a child might adopt the belief that they don't need to express gratitude for their education because their parents have already paid for it. This mentality is akin to transactional interactions in a market, where neither the customer nor the shopkeeper typically express gratitude for the exchange of goods and money. However, it's worth considering what might happen if gratitude were expressed in such situations. Just as purchasing a pair of comfortable shoes provides relief through their use rather than by simply possessing money, expressing gratitude acknowledges the value of the service or product received. While the customer benefits from the purchase, the shopkeeper also benefits from the transaction as it helps meet their financial needs and supports their livelihood. In life, there are numerous needs and exchanges beyond material goods, and expressing gratitude can enhance the quality of these interactions, fostering mutual appreciation and understanding.

The question is - what would be the impact on others if we offer gratitude. Let me start with a story.

Once, an angel traversed a desert and encountered a distressed bird suffering from dehydration amidst the barren landscape. Curious about the angel's destination, the bird inquired if he was en route to see God. The angel confirmed this and upon the bird's request, promised to inquire about the duration of her suffering. Upon returning from the divine encounter, the angel relayed to the bird that while her situation seemed bleak, she should cultivate gratitude for every blessing received. He revealed that her current plight stemmed from a past life where she had neglected expressions of gratitude, leading to her present predicament. In a subsequent visit, the angel was astonished to find the once-suffering bird now flourishing amidst lush greenery, happily chirping away. Inquiring of this transformation, God revealed that it was a result of the bird's newfound attitude of gratitude. This revelation underscored the significance of expressing gratitude, even in divine eyes.

There are three R's to offer gratitude. These are to Recognise, to Remember and to Reciprocate. Let us take these one by one. Once you start expressing gratitude, you would feel an added joy. "**Gratitude and love are always multiplied when you give freely. Gratitude is an infinite source of contentment and energy**." The need is to Recognise. Let us probe further. How many times have you offered gratitude to your parents for bringing you up, nurturing, paying for your school fees, your clothes and your other requirements? How many times have you offered thanks to GOD for giving you this beautiful world to live? God has given us the eyes to see, ears to listen to music, nose to smell, tongue to taste and hands to touch. Just try to offer thanks for seeing anything pleasing, for listening to good music and for having a chance to taste so many good dishes daily. Since you get everything without paying any price for the same, you start taking it as your right. If unfortunately any of the privileges is withdrawn, you start cursing GOD for it. So recognize the facilities provided by someone to you , maybe silently. Second R is to Remember. Whosoever does some favour to you, you have to remember him. If you do not, you will be considered a thankless person. Today, wherever you are, it is because of the efforts done by your teachers and your parents for you. Third R is to Reciprocate. If you remember all the good work done by someone, there are chances to pass it to someone else and a chain reaction will start. This is going to add more happiness and more love in your heart and this world would be a beautiful place to live in. Sometimes it is not possible to pay back to the same person from whom you got the favour. No problem, you can pay back the same to some other person or even to the same person at a later stage, when you become more resourceful. It would be possible only if you Recognize as well as Remember. This is going to add to your happiness too.

You may be thinking that you are too young and your resources are too meagre and it is not possible for you to reciprocate. But you can recognize and remember and can offer gratitude mentally through "thoughts" and "words". A day may come when you can reciprocate through your deeds as well. It is a win-win situation for both, one who offers and the one who accepts. Even in day to day life, if your friend helps you in any way, you must thank him. Make it a habit. This habit is going to make you popular in your circle. People will like your company. It is a real service to mankind and is very essential in day to day life. Just introspect about the number of persons who are helping you to lead a peaceful and comfortable life. Offer gratitude
- to the farmer who is growing food for you
- to the soldier who saves you from enemies attack
- to the building contractor who made a beautiful house for you to live in
- to the labourer who has done work in building the house
- to the tailor who stitches your clothes.
There are so many people in this world who are making your life comfortable. Your parents, teachers, mentors, friends - all are helping you to live a better life. Imagine a situation when you have a lot of money in your hand but you are cut off from this world. What can you do with that money? Be ready to pay gratitude to all those who help you in your day to day life. Only then you may be considered as a human in true sense otherwise you will be in the category of animals. Get down on your knees and thank God for everything.

Assets :
Inquisitive Questions
1) When you get a prize in your annual function, what do you say to the guest when he gives the prize to you?
2) Why should you offer gratitude?

3) How many people are there in the world to whom you owe gratitude?

4) Have you ever offered gratitude to your parents for so much they have done for you?

5) If you get some work done by some person on payment basis, even then you should offer gratitude. Do you agree with this? Why?

Interesting Asides

Gratitude is the investment which increases once you offer it to someone. It gets multiplied when shared.

Suggestive Activity

Dear Children, Close your eyes, listen to me carefully and pray silently. Thank you God that you have given me another day to enjoy. Thank you God that you have given me enough space to sleep in a nice bed room. Thank you God for providing me with a good uniform to go to the school. Thank you God for providing me a good school for my studies - a school which is providing me value based education. Thank you God for providing me with good teachers to prepare me for the exam of life. Thank you God for giving me many friends to play with. Thank you GOD for giving me the ability to understand. Thank You GOD for helping me out to face any situation and for giving me enough courage to bear any loss. Thank You God for giving me energy to digest food. Thank you GOD for providing me strength to work for making myself comfortable. Dear children, now open your eyes and just recall the thanks due to GOD.

Day to Day Relevance

When we offer gratitude to someone, we get the same from that person in return. It is an activity which provides happiness to both, the one who offers and the one to whom it is offered.

Value Content

As humans, we should exhibit greater wisdom than animals. While a dog expresses gratitude by wagging its tail when given food, we possess the capacity for deeper understanding and appreciation.

Questions to Assess

1) Should we offer gratitude just because of the fear of losing a relationship?
2) Offering gratitude is a physical activity or mental too?
3) Name a person, who does not offer gratitude to any one?
4) How will you offer your gratitude to GOD before going to sleep?
5) Create a sentence/paragraph for offering gratitude from morning till evening.

Day 25
Stress Management

With the passage of time and the changing world, it is the stress which is on the rise. Stress is the symptom of negativity which indicates that some changes are required in the present system. Little stress is required to go. When stress starts, our body generates some hormones and it gives enough energy to manage the stress, but when it crosses the limit (it becomes injurious to health) that it even reaches to suicidal attempts in some cases. Present generation is not well equipped with the techniques of managing stress. Everyone is running fast and there is no time to look back. No one is there to support the one who lags behind. We are missing love for GOD and have no respect for the law of the society. We are lacking patience and faith. Stress is the cause of many diseases like cancer, heart diseases and hypertension. It is becoming difficult with each passing day to get a good job and even if you get a good job, there is no security. The gap between the rich and the poor is increasing. Middle class families are decreasing. Desire is multiplying exponentially. Even the children, who used to be stress free earlier, are now coming in the grip of stress. A six year old child is also suffering because of anxiety which is close to stress.

The parents may be responsible for this occurrence and generation of stress in their children. Now-a-days, there are only one or two children in nuclear families and parents want to fulfil their dreams only through them. Real problem starts when their dreams and the interests of the child clash. The quality time spent together with parents and children, especially adolescents, no longer exists. As a result, there are many issues that are stressful for the adolescents but can be easily resolved by the parents. But due to not sharing the issues, the stress level is multiplying. Differences because of the generation gap are on the increase. As the train of life is moving fast, it has become difficult for everyone to catch up. It is very common to read in the newspapers that several children end their life because of petty issues. The simple reason behind these suicides is that the stress level in them reaches very high and they find no solution to their problems. Because of this, cases of depression are increasing day by day and very soon, over 50% of the problems would be stress related only. We need to discuss some techniques to manage the stress levels. Let us discuss these one by one.

First technique is 4Cs. These C's are **Challenge, Cope, Control** and **Communicate**. You should learn to take every problem as a challenge (1st 'C'). Accept the challenge as it is. We have discussed earlier, how to face the challenge. It is the same as if we are facing the devil inside. To implement this C, we can use 4F formula, i.e. Follow the master, Face the challenge, Fight till end and Finish the game. Instead of taking problems very seriously and with a heavy heart, think that this is a way of life and the road of life is not so smooth. As per Swami Vivekananda ***'the day you have no problem is the day wasted'.*** Imagine that you are going on a road and a dog starts barking at you. If you start running, it is almost sure that the dog will also run after you, but once you face it, it will be scared and will not follow you. Similarly if you take the problem as a challenge and prepare yourself to face the same, your stress level will automatically go down.

Second "C" is "Cope". You should not change your routine work because of any problem. It is observed that some people do not eat or sleep properly when they face any problem and in that case, their stress increases. Better keep your routine intact and prepare yourself for the worst. Your routine should remain as it is – be it taking the bath, doing exercises, eating or sleeping. Third "C" is "control", i.e. whatever control is possible, must be done. Suppose you have to appear for an examination tomorrow and you have still to revise the whole book, you feel stressed. Instead of worrying, it is always better to prepare whatever chapters you can. Out of the total problems, there is always some part for which the solution is in your hands. At least, try to manage that much so that the problem reduces to some extent. Still if it is not manageable, do not keep it with you. Here comes the 4th 'C'. i.e. Communicate. Share it with someone who is close to you but do not share it with all. If the problem is not worth sharing with any one, share it with GOD. Sit somewhere and just talk to GOD as if you are talking to some person. If 4Cs are properly followed religiously, you will be relieved to a great extent.

Accept the problem, listen to it, introspect and write it down. Sometimes you are unable to identify the problem, but it is at your subconscious level and by introspecting, you will be able to find out the solution. You will find that when the stress is building up, then there is no harmony of thoughts, words and deeds. Heart and head fight with each other. Remember that the past is past and the future is uncertain, so live in the present. This is the solution to the problem. Merely by running away from the problem will not solve it. Sometimes we are afraid of the criticism, thinking what others will say about our actions. Simply we become over conscious and this creates stress. Better listen to your master, your super- conscious mind and act accordingly. Do your duty and leave the rest to GOD. Rather learn the art of surrendering to GOD. Your critics are your best friends. They would give you the vision to fight. Do not give your remote control to someone else. If someone praises you, you feel happy and if someone criticizes you, you feel sad. People do not take others as seriously as you think. Your life is yours and you should be the architecture of your own destiny. Develop self-confidence. Start with a small venture first. Suppose you decide to take a bath with cold water one day in winter and keep doing it thereafter. This small venture will raise your self-confidence and will help you in stress management. You should love yourself first. Remember that your competition is with you only. You have to compete with yourself first. Stress starts when you start copying others. GOD has created you as a unique piece and there is no carbon copy of yours existing in this world.

Develop positive thinking. It is possible by keeping good company. Even some good books can also help you. Here I would like to mention a book written by Dale Carnaige titled **"How to stop worrying and start living"**. Many of the problems are our own creation and many of the events do not happen as we think. Just check the probability of the event and check how many times in the past this has happened? Sometimes stress is due to conflicts with your friends. Sometimes you may be at fault and sometimes your friend may be. Sometimes this situation of conflict is created by someone else. Better resolve the issue at the earliest. If you are at fault, ask for forgiveness and if he/she is at fault, forgive him/her. If someone else is at fault, meet him, clarify the matter and resolve the issues. We sometimes lie and create a situation ourselves to come under stress with the fear of being caught.

The stress is mainly because of your own nature. It does not depend on any situation, instead it depends upon your own ways of thinking. Better plan to eradicate this devil. Contemplate on this issue. Learn meditation, read good books, join some club, go close to the nature, do exercises and change your habits. It is possible to change this habit at your age, but may not be possible at a later stage.

Assets:
Inquisitive questions
1) What is stress? Do you think stress always plays a negative role or is it a necessary evil?
2) What are the main reasons for getting stressed? Do you think anxiety is one of the reasons for stress?
3) What do you consider as your stress buster?
4) Can you recognize your friends who are under stress?
5) Should you hide stress from your parents?

6) What are the side effects of stress?
7) Identify any situation when you are stressed.

Interesting Asides

Laughter is the best stress buster even if there is no reason to laugh. Even artificial laughter serves the purpose because the subconscious mind cannot distinguish between natural and artificial laughter.

An interesting joke on Stress relief:
Doctor: What do you do when you feel stressed?
Patient: I go to the temple...
Doctor: Good... and you pray there?
Patient: No... I mix-up all shoes kept outside and watch people more stressed than me... and my stress goes away.

Suggestive Activity

1) Go to some nearby park when you are under stress and stay there for half an hour observing and appreciating nature. Check if your stress level has reduced.
2) Observe, if helping some underprivileged reduces your stress.

Day to Day Relevance

When you are under stress, the glossy look of your face is lost. Sometimes the stress gets converted into headache and it gets multiplied. If someone is under stress, it is better to leave him/her alone for some time. Wait till the person under stress wants to share the reasons for his/her stress.

Value Content

Prayer is a tonic for the removal of stress. Say prayer and surrender to GOD.

Questions to Assess

1) What are the main reasons for the occurrence of stress?
2) Why are children too facing stress these days?
3) When is the stress required? Explain the situation.
4) Do you think alcohol reduces stress?
5) Is stress hereditary?

Day 26
Change Management

The world is changing very fast. We, the teachers and people of our generation have seen many changes happen around us. We saw an era of black and white TV with one interesting programme, which was "Chitarhar" with old songs and also some old movies on Sunday. But, what is the situation now? Anyone who wants to watch TV 24 by 7, can do so easily as there are a lot of channels with a variety of programmes and one can continue watching for hours together. Not only the TV, the communication technology too has drastically changed over a period. We used to ring telephone exchanges to ask for a local number and now we can see even the clear picture and actions of our friends or relatives sitting in Japan or any other place in the world. You saw that Japan used cars without drivers and robots to lift the luggage of the visitors during the 2020 Olympics. How can we depend upon the age-old methods of learning?

In today's rapidly evolving world, adaptability is paramount for survival. As Charles Darwin once stated, "It is not the most intelligent nor the strongest species that will survive, but the one who is most responsive to change." The current era, or "Yug" is characterized by constant technological advancements. Could one imagine life without the Internet today? The answer is a resounding "NO," yet just 25 years ago, the Internet was not widely accessible, and people managed without it.

Numerous facets of life have undergone significant transformations. Banking systems, ticket booking, shopping methods with online platforms, photography techniques, education systems, communication methods, medical science and treatments, transportation systems, gaming, irrigation techniques, lifestyle, and management strategies—all have been subject to change. "Change" is an ongoing process, and one must adapt to these shifts to thrive in this dynamic environment.

Just imagine a bank with an old system of maintaining manual ledgers. Imagine what would happen if the manual ledger gets burnt in a fire. Imagine the old system of railway ticket booking – where you used to stand in a queue for over 6 hours to get a ticket reserved. In 1988, I myself had waited in a queue for over 5 hours to get a train ticket. For a particular train, there used to be only one window and now, you can book a ticket for any train, any day and from anywhere – even from the comfort of your home. Previously, when seeking information on a specific topic, one would typically consult various books or experts before acquiring any insights. However, with the advent of technology, accessing a wealth of information has become as easy as clicking a mouse button on your laptop. Google's search engine, often referred to as "Google Baba," has made this process incredibly convenient, providing an ocean of information at one's fingertips.

Imagine when you were travelling to some unknown city or village and you were to reach a particular house, you would have asked several people for the location of that house. But now, the GPS system in your mobile phone leads you to that house without asking anyone. Imagine the use of cameras where you would put a reel, click photos, get it developed and then get the prints out. How tedious and costly the affair was! And now, you have the mobile phone with high quality in-built cameras. You can click N number of photos anywhere without any setup and with zero cost. Two decades earlier, many people suffering from cancer or other such fatal diseases used to die as there was no cure for such ailments. But now, there is hardly any death reported from such deadly and chronic diseases. Your great grand-father would not have even dreamt to travel from Delhi to Washington, but now anyone can travel easily. Aren't these changes mind blowing? What would happen if you don't adapt to these changes and continue to stick to the old methods? I have narrated only a few examples of the changes we notice in our life, but CHANGE is an on-going process in every walk of our life.

Human nature often resists change, yet the reality remains: one must adapt or face dire consequences. Change can be categorized as either predictable or unpredictable. Predictable changes allow for preparation as one is aware of the impending shift. Conversely, unpredictable changes catch us off guard, leaving us mentally unprepared. In such situations, bravery is essential as we must face these changes head-on, adjusting and acting accordingly. The Response to any Change is either Forced or Voluntary.

There are hard as well as soft aspects of any Change. Hard aspects are easy to create like Roles, Equipment, Structure and Systems. Soft aspects are a bit difficult to create and include Motivation, Involvement, Commitment, Passion and Ambition. There are certain prerequisites to Change management and these include:
1. Vision
2. Readiness
3. Ambition
4. Innovation
5. Commitment
6. Knowledge
7. Learning (from failures)
8. Alignment (organization, people, customers, technology)
9. Mind-set

The challenge lies in navigating the fast-paced race of the contemporary world. As time progresses, the rate of change is expected to accelerate even further than it is today. Emerging technologies will continue to evolve, playing a crucial role in benefiting humanity when used effectively. I will summarize this topic of Change Management into following steps:
1. Change Happens and will continue to happen – Accept the change
2. Anticipate the Change

3. Monitor the Change
4. Adapt quickly to the Change
5. Change yourself
6. Enjoy the Change
7. Be ready to Change quickly and enjoy it again.

There have been two fundamental changes that have changed the entire world - LPG (Liberalization/Privatization/Globalization) and ICT (Information and Communication Technology). We will not go into the in-depth discussions of these at this stage but you may study these in detail on your own. I may conclude this lesson with two powerful quotes:

- "When the winds of change blow, most build shelter to protect themselves; some build windmills to take advantage of the change".
- "Be the change that you wish to see in the world" – Mahatma Gandhi.

Assets :
Inquisitive Questions
1) What is a Change and why should you adopt it?
2) What will a Change mean to you?
3) How will a change impact you?
4) Why do people resist Change?
5) What if you are forced to do more for the same pay?

Interesting Asides
1) "www" is generally the short form of "World Wide Web". But I consider it as the short form of "Winning Ways at Work". This is the change in thinking.
2) Just play the song "Nadiya chale, chale re dhara, tujhko chalna hoga". Explain its next line i.e. "tu na chalega to chal dengi rahen, manzil ko tarsengi teri nigahen ".

Suggestive Activity

1) Identify three key things you have learnt from this lesson which you can use in your day-to-day work. Identify any change that happened in your life which you did not like but were forced to adopt it.

2) You have been studying in DC Model School for the last 5 years and have been recognized as a brilliant child by school management and the teachers. Your house is just a 5 minute walk from your school. Imagine that your parents got transferred to Mumbai and you got admission in a school in Mumbai located at a distance of about 15 km from your new house. Your location has changed, your principal and teachers have changed and your friends have changed. Describe this change in detail as to what difficulties you had to face and how you overcame these.

Day to Day Relevance

Living in a comfort zone makes you happy and you want to hold on to this situation. But, if you do not change, you become extinct. Keep observing the changes around you and move beyond your fear. The quicker you let go of your comfort zone, the sooner you find a new world and new opportunities. Old beliefs do not lead you to new situations.

There are many people who change their cars after every 3 to 4 years, just for the sake of change. Similarly, ladies change the setting of their house just to make it appealing to the eyes for the sake of fun.

Value Content

Be, Do and Tell.

Accepting Small Changes early helps you adapt to the Bigger Changes that are yet to come. We must move with the changes and enjoy it.

Questions to Assess

1) There have been big companies like PAL, Zenith, Forhans etc. Why have they failed?
2) What are the benefits of supporting a Change?
3) What is the rush for you to change?
4) What is the risk or the potential consequences of not changing?
5) What are your choices during a change process?
6) Why do employees or teachers become stressed and distracted from day-to-day work?
7) Imagine the world after 10 years. What kind of changes do you expect? (HOT).

Go Green

Till now, we have been only telling you what not to do. Let us now discuss what to do? After so many years of independence, we still carry our mind set that reducing pollution is the work of the government and not ours. Now we will have to think rationally as to how we can help our government? Just see the present state of affairs. Our capital is 30 times more polluted than the limit given by WHO. Still we do not mind celebrating Diwali with crackers. We are adding fuel to fire. Yes, there are many factors which are responsible for the increasing pollution. And still we have not yet planned for any effective system of garbage disposal. In the name of Swachha Bharat, we simply throw the garbage into a dustbin and feel that our duty is over. Rest, the government should look after. We can put some effort into reducing the garbage. There are many items that can be recycled. Get those items recycled and save money for our country. We can reuse the empty shaving and toothpaste tubes. If we are aware of the recycling process, our garbage will be reduced by 50% and hence our problem of disposal will also be reduced substantially.

See the kind of exploitation we are doing with the 5 elements. Let us take one by one. First element is the **SKY**. See how much sound vibrations are we producing and these are increasing rapidly. Every mobile phone is emitting vibrations. There are now mobile towers being constructed everywhere and because of the vibrations emitted through these towers, some of the small birds are getting extinct. There does not seem to be any chance of reducing these vibrations. Most of us are now using the internet and Wi-Fi for various activities throughout the day. With the three primary necessary requirements of bread, clothing and shelter (ROTI KAPDA aur MAKAAN), another addition is the internet for the youth and is probably the most essential now. If for any reason, there is a failure in the availability of the internet, they start suffocating as if they cannot survive without it. We need urgent solutions to reduce this problem.

Second element of priority is the **AIR**. Now every house of 4 members has 5 cars. Each member wants to drive his own car without thinking of the fuel consumption. We do not understand the fact that we may afford it but our nation cannot. The smoke emitted from the industries is increasing day by day. Ours is a developing country and we have a dream of making the products of our own, instead of importing the goods. Good, it will save our revenue, but what about the pollution? The quantity of carbon dioxide is increasing day by day. What kind of precautions should you take to avoid the pollution? There seems to be no easy solution. Number of asthmatic patients is increasing every day. Metropolitan cities are worse and the children are suffering a lot. Elders still have the immunity, but what about the younger ones who are yet to develop immunity? Medical expenses are on the rise. Poor people are unable to bear the burden of medicines and hospitals. There is no substitute for the thermal plants for generating electricity. The situation of increasing pollution gets worse during paddy season, when farmers burn the residual left. Since there is no economical substitute available, nothing is working out. Everyone is bound to inhale the polluted air.

Our 3rd element is the **FIRE**. Due to the industrialization and cutting of the trees, atmospheric temperature is on the rise. With the rise of temperature, glaciers are melting. The water level at the sea is on rise. There is a danger of submerging cities around the sea as the ecological balance is getting destroyed. It seems as if the GOD forgot the timings of the seasons to change. Rains are as unpredictable as the winter and summer seasons. The use of Air Conditioners (AC) has increased manifold. People are becoming more comfortable. Earlier an AC was used to be a commodity in MNC offices only, now it has entered every house and is becoming the main source of global warming. There is a hole in the ozone layer which is used to protect us from the harmful sun rays. Many people are suffering from skin diseases. Every person wants to be allowed to enjoy modern gadgets and GOD should take care of global warming. To meet the demands of the society, trees are being cut. People are becoming more selfish. Even the farmers are converting their agricultural land to industrial purpose which is more economical for them. Ecologist's warnings have no effect on the people. Many of us think that nothing is going to happen if I alone will avoid using the AC or try to reduce global warming.

The 4th element is the **WATER**. There is too much water pollution now. Every river is facing the problem of pollution. Industrialists are throwing their garbage in rivers without treating it with some treatment plant. The TDS of drinking water is now crossing 300 mark whereas it should have been 50 as per WHO. Many of the people are using RO to reduce the TDS (RO makes the TDS to almost zero). But because of the lack of knowledge, they are comfortable with a zero TDS in water, which is again harmful. The use of water bottles is on the rise in every occasion or gathering. People, after using the water, throw away the bottles, which again is adding to the garbage. These water bottles are kept open while transporting from one place to another and get exposed to the heat of the sun. The heat of the sun with plastic is making the water polluted and is a source of cancer. People are suffering from this deadly disease without knowing the origin of it. Youth especially like to drink chilled water and avoid using pot water which once was considered to be extremely healthy. Every house is keeping refrigerators and freezers and we are living to drink and not drinking to live. Because of the polluted water, many fishes die every day. The water of rivers and the oceans is so polluted that it is not even worth bathing. Disposing garbage in the rivers is a usual practice and a lot of polythene is also thrown in the rivers creating a permanent problem. Government is spending so much to clean the rivers, but without changing our mind set, nothing will be possible in this direction.

The 5th element is our mother **EARTH**. To get better yield, farmers are using the fertilizer much more than what is required. Lot of urea is seen in the milk because the cows are using the same grass with a high quantity of urea. The soil is getting polluted day by day. There is no system of garbage disposal. People are habitual of passing by the garbage heaps with a stinking smell. Every village has similar scenes. Even cities are no exception. We have so many beautiful places to see and can attract outsiders. This can be a source of revenue generation but it is extremely sorry to say that no one is maintaining them. Even the walls of monuments are in bad shape with writing of useless remarks. People are afraid of diseases and avoid visiting our country. We are not maintaining our hill stations. People, being selfish, are making it more and more congested. The purpose of visiting a hill station has been ruined.

Now the problem is that we cannot think of living without all the comforts and the facilities that the modern world has given to us. Is there any solution for it? We have discussed these problems many times through declamation and debates. It appears now as if we have no harmony of thought, word and deed. There is a solution with you also and the solution is to **Go Green**. Just think, what is going to happen if we grow more trees? Like human beings, the trees also need the sky to grow. We pollute the sky with vibrations, our negative thoughts and our abusive language etc. While the trees absorb these vibrations to some extent and thus repay back their loan towards the sky. Then there is the air which we need to live in. We pollute the air by consuming oxygen from air and convert the same to carbon dioxide while trees take in the carbon dioxide and give back the oxygen. We need approximately 2 lakh rupees to generate the same amount of oxygen which one tree produces. Our third element is FIRE. Trees are the only source of reducing global warming. There is no other solution except to grow trees and to reduce our wants, which I fear, we will not reduce. Fourth element is water. We use water and pay back to earth in the form of urine. We consume pure water and make it dirty while trees use dirty water and give it back in the form of juices. Fifth is our earth, which we are polluting with our garbage. If we use it judicially and use the leaves of trees and the fertilizers properly, we can reduce the earth pollution too. The important point is that GOD has given this right to humans to get rid of our debt of polluting nature, which unfortunately we are not doing. We must start working on it. Let us be aware of this problem and just visualize its consequences. Otherwise, our next generation is going to suffer because of our foolishness. The children should be made aware of this problem and each one of us should work to pay back the nature. What have we taken from the 5 elements? No doubt, we cannot do as much as the trees can, but trees cannot grow on their own. They need our help. This is the best opportunity provided by GOD to us. Let us avail this and get rid of the obligation of nature to us, if not fully, at least partially.

Assets :

Inquisitive Questions

1) How many elements are present in nature? Can we manage without any one?
2) Do you agree that the quality of the 5 elements is going down with the passage of time?
3) Do we have any other option except to use all the five elements for our personal use or can we not raise the quality of at least one of the 5 elements of our own? Explain.
4) Why do you go to a hill station during vacations?
5) Which is the main reason for the pollution - selfishness of people or reduction in sources? Explain.
6) What you think is the role of the government to reduce the problem of pollution.

Suggestive Activity
- Draw a chart and paste it in the corridor and at some common places to remind us of our duties towards nature (priority wise).

- List down the activities that you can take up to reduce the pollution. Study for a week about the implementation of the listed activities. Also note if there is any change, you observe.

Day to Day Relevance

We have the same ratio of elements inside us as it is outside. The illness is because when the ratio inside or outside varies.

We can make our place cool by growing more trees. By growing 50,000 more trees in our town, we can reduce the summer temperature by one degree and increase the chances of increasing the rain by 20%.

Value Content

You can help the society with growing more trees and making Nature happy.

Questions to Assess

1) What are the reasons for our falling ill?
2) How can we reduce global warming?
3) What will happen if glaciers melt?
4) What can we do if we have no space to grow trees?
5) Ceiling on desires can help to reduce the problem of pollution. Explain.
6) If the glaciers are melting, why is the underground water level of earth not increasing? (HOT).

Day 28
Life is a Game, Play it

Dear Children,

To have mastery of games, we need to understand the reward and punishment aspect of the game. Life itself is a game. Everyone entertains a good player and vice versa is also true. Which side would you like to choose, i.e. good player where everyone welcomes you or otherwise, I know your answer. Everyone would like to be demanding. Everyone would like to be recognised. Sometimes for recognition we choose unfair means but very soon you will be shunted out, if you continue doing the same. Better go for a permanent solution. You should be a genuine player. For getting recognition you will have to sacrifice the comfort zone and will have to develop habit of a fighter. Who is restricting you to be a fighter equipped with all the quality of a good player? You will have to read out the manual of life and will have to follow the instructions religiously and learn the art of living. Let us understand the salient features of game first. When we play a game:

1. Each Player is given equal opportunities and no discrimination is made. One may be rich or poor, game is game and everyone is same for the organiser. Sometimes you feel that the other one is favoured but actually it is your own deposits and withdrawals and organiser acts as a bank manager and pays back whatever you have earned.

2. There is a fixed boundary where game is played. Crossing the boundary is noticed. In one game crossing the boundary may give you an extra point and in the other it may be called penalty. But for a particular game it is same and will

not change. You are supposed to follow the limit setup by the manager.

3. In a game your individual as well as team performance is seen. You are to act accordingly and take decision accordingly. Outsider will make judgement and will assess your performance accordingly.

4. There is an opposite team with whom you are to fight. More force is required to win over the opposite team if opposition is stronger. Patience and perseverance are required to win over the game.

5. It is not always that you will win; there are days when you face defeat too. But defeating once or twice is not end. Game continues if you get up for next bout. You need to learn with every bout and you will be considered real loser when you give up mentally. Never, ever give up.

6. A good player always introspects after the game and tries to see his/her mistakes and promises not to repeat them next time. This learning of lesson continues.

7. There are referees who do not participate in game but make judgement and give you tips after the game, only if you ask for. It is advisable to ask the referees about your strength and weakness and follow the advice.

8. When you are winner, many others will congratulate you and would like to show their association with you. You will be welcomed by all. If you lose the game, many will be there to criticise and very few will be available to wipe away your tears. You need to keep equilibrium and not to get elated when you win and not to get depressed when you lose.

9. The number of people greeting you depends upon how big your victory is. It is better to offer your sincere gratitude to your master who taught you the rules of game and not to gain ego when you win.

Your question will be why I am telling you all about the game. Dear, I want you to introspect that in life we are also playing a game. Consciously or unconsciously, in our game of life all the rules are applied. Let us check one by one:

1. Every one of us is given two eyes, two ears, one mouth and one nose by God irrespective of rich or poor to work with. All are given 24 hours a day. Some of us complain to God for not providing enough resources and others are comfortable in comparison to us without knowing the inner story. Instead, we should assess our own strength and work hard to compete ourselves without feeling jealous of others. It is the first mantra to be a good player.

2. Our boundary is fixed. Our eyes can see same distance, our hearing power is limited and limit up to which we can eat is also fixed. Whenever we cross the limit, we are warned by the referees and the third eye installed in the field of game. Overeating, overviewing, over listening are noticed and as per the offence, yellow, red card is shown. If still we continue crossing the limit, we are sent back to pavilion. We are to wait for the next game after learning the lesson. Some of us get mental defeat and blame someone else for our mistake.

3. Some of the jobs are assigned individually. No one else can eat in our place. No one else can share our pain, our illness. Some of the jobs depend on others too. Food we eat is sown by someone (farmer), sold by another and consumed by someone else. It is like passing the parcel.

4. There is an opposition everywhere. You are to win over the opposition. In the game of life, our mind is the opponent, we know what is right and what is wrong theoretically but our mind acts as an opponent. We have to master the mind and be a mastermind.

5. Ups and downs are there. Sometime our super-consciousness (which is real I) wins and sometimes we lose too. But this game continues. We need to give strength to our super-conscious mind by nurturing it with vitamin "M" i.e. Meditation so that probability of winning should be more. Still not to get discouraged when the game is lost. Learn from the mistakes and continue your game.

6. If you are a good player, you sit at peace and visualise what went wrong (WWW). You plan with yourself not to repeat it again. You notice the triggers and try to find the solution for the same. Noticing triggers means what prompted your monkey mind to go in the wrong direction (instead of doing goal to your opponent, you goal to the wrong end). If you are a bad player, you try to put blame on others for your failure.

7. You are given a super-conscious mind as a referee, always ready to guide you, provided you ask. Unfortunately, you make it dormant by ignoring it and never ask the referee and gradually you lose the favour of the referee.

8. When you do hard work and get success, there are many who congratulate you but when you fail, very few are there to console and uplift you. You should understand this universal truth and have discriminating power to judge to whom you should trust and who your real friend is.

9. If you do something great, quality of work will decide your achievement. If you get first position in class, your teacher, your parents and your principal will congratulate you. If you secure any position in district many more will be added and excellence has no limit. It depends; how big your achievement is. Recognition is directly proportional to the level of your success.

To play the game of life you need to be vigilant. ABC of game is Always be Careful, Avoid bad company and Always be cheerful. After every round ask yourself, have you played your game nicely? Where did you commit the mistake? How to rectify next time? What was triggering? How to save yourself for the next time? Be in learning mode always as good players do. Not to be egoistic if you and your team win and not to be disheartened if you lose, as real loss is when you lose mentally. If you get up after every bout and introspect every time and apply 4F (already explained) with 2P (Patience and Perseverance) applying 4C (Challenge, Cope, Control and Communicate), you will be a good player. Learn from the mistake but do not stick up with guilt. Past is past, now live in the present as future will be shaped with your present learning. You have enough time to shape your destiny, provided you do not postpone and wait for someone. If you feel someone will come and provide you a magical wand to excel and door of success will open for you, then you are mistaken as it will open only when you knock the door. Manual of life is there; you need to read the autobiography of the others who have achieved the target with their hard work. Concluding this with famous quote of Vivekananda: "Arise, awake and stop not till you achieve your goal".

Assets :

Inquisitive Questions:

1. What do you mean by the game?
2. Is life a game?
3. Why should we play the game, i.e. what will happen if we stop playing?
4. Can a person of 60+ ages play the game? What kind of precautions should a 60+ take?

Suggestive Activity:
Make a chart of games and prove that there is a game fixed for everyone and prove that there is no one in the world who cannot play. Of course, one will have to adjust the game as per one's capability.

Value Content:
Your game should be a source of entertainment to others and you should follow two principles while playing "Love all and serve all" and "Help ever, hurt never".

Interesting aside:
Name of persons who have played the game of life by putting their 100% are written in the world book and it is a source of inspiration for the next generation. Interesting part is that there are hardly a few whose records are still not beaten by anyone, otherwise there is always someone who is there to replace.

Day to Day Relevance:
Game is essential for everyone to play. If you find someone who stops playing, you will observe that society discards them. They are no longer a positive thinker.

Questions to Assess:
1. What is the difference between the game we play in the ground and game of life?
2. While playing the game of life, what special care will you take i.e. which is different from our normal games?
3. When someone stops playing and retires, what kind of changes occurs?
4. As per the Geeta, there is no one in the world that is not playing. How far do you agree with this? (HOT).

Day 29
When you cross the limit

Dear Children,
Let me tell you what the meaning of crossing the limit is? Universal truth is that from the ancient time you are witnessing a tug of war between good and bad. The same war is there inside us too. At one end there is Super-conscious mind as a symbol of wisdom and goodness and at the other end there is sub-conscious mind as a symbol of worldly pleasure prompting us most of the time to cross the limit. Conscious mind alerts and sets the balance between the two but when you stop feeding your super-conscious mind and finally your super-conscious mind becomes dormant and sometimes almost dead, sub-conscious mind becomes powerful and start doing whatsoever it wishes. Crossing the limit is when you feed your sub-conscious mind with junk food for eyes, ears, nose and tongue and you even stop listening to your conscious mind too. A stage comes when you decide to run away from realities and land into trouble. It is already covered in chapter--- of LOC.

This chapter is for the advance story, i.e. what happens when you cross the limit. You ran away from realities and most of the time you alone don't cross the limit but take away some of the likeminded friends of yours along with you. Yours sub-conscious mind takes you away to the fairy land of imagination where you visualise as if by crossing the limit, all your worries of studies, scolding of parents and teachers will disappear and you will be happy all the way. You will do whatever you wish to do and visualise that you will get rid of all problems and it will be a place of comfort and happiness and whole of the world will help you to enjoy your so-called freedom. It is like a kite which thinks that this string by which it is bound is not letting it enjoy the life and kite does not visualise its fate once it manages to stay at the height without string. Dear children, without thinking the consequences of your fate, your sub-conscious mind puts you into deep trouble. It is like crossing the Laxman Rekha by Sita. You know the story of Ramayana and you must know that her intention was pure while crossing the limit set up by Laxman for her, still she could not pacify the society. How much you suffer when you cross the limit, let us discuss it.

1. You cannot imagine the suffering of your parents especially mother and she remains in pains till you do not come back. It may be a pleasure trip for you but for your parents it is so horrible and they pass painful sleepless nights till they receive news of your safety.
2. Your school suffers a lot. There are many rumours attached. Media takes it as an opportunity and makes it box news for the next day. Parents sometimes start blaming school teachers and classmates without thinking of consequences of the same. Reputation of school suffers and it is tough time for teachers, principal and Management of school too. Police enters the school premises and lot of queries from other parents of the school start.
3. School will have financial losses too, as people will think twice before admitting. Other schools will not hesitate telling this to others that children of this school are under the influence of drugs. Your crossing the limit will spoil the image of other children of the school too. It is the universal truth that when someone crosses the limit, society applies it to the entire stakeholder. Its vice versa is also true, when any child gets recognition in academic, sports and other co-curricular activities credit too is given to other stakeholders. No one likes to keep a child like you to school as it will be

control the damage further. You or your parents may give a guarantee but no one would like to spare you as school would like to give lesson to others so that no one else repeats the same.

4. Even your pleasure is temporary and very soon you too realise that you have committed the blunder. If it is night time it gets aggravated, where to stay at night and it gets multiplied if it is winter.

5. This stigma of crossing the limit will be with you forever, even when you become a parent. Now you are child, you seek your parents as a role model, tomorrow when you will be the parent, you should be role model of your children. Imagine how heavy the penalty is.

6. Tomorrow others may hesitate sitting with you as you and your friends will be tagged as a bad company.

7. You will curse yourself when you will peep into your past, i.e. a sense of guilt will always disturb you.

Assets :

Inquisitive Questions:

1. How far do you agree that this body is a limited company?

2. Have you ever thought of running away from your home and try to do something extra ordinary when you listen to the success stories of some of the actors?

3. Have you ever tried over-eating while attending any marriage party?

4. What happens when you continuously watch T.V. for more than 8 hours or listen to musical songs?

Suggested Activity:

Imagine the situation when your parent gives you 5000 rupees and make you free and ask you to do whatever you wish, go wherever you want to go, what will be your plan? Discuss which better, Independence or Inner dependence is. You can have debate by making two teams, one in favour of independence and other one in favour of inner dependence.

Value Content:
You are independent till your independence does not disturb others. Wait for the day when God gives you chance to cross the limit.

Day to Day Relevance:
Limit of Every one is fixed
1. Teacher is given fixed space in the form of black-Board and cannot write beyond Black Board.
2. God has given us a fix audibility range beyond the same we cannot listen.
3. The boundary of every game is fixing, if you catch the ball beyond the boundary, player will not be considered out.

Interesting Aside:
Although God has fixed the limit of everything but still to make the game interesting the limit of desire is not fixed. Once one desire is full filled another desire crops in. Whosoever becomes an obstacle becomes our enemy.

Questions to Assess:
1. As a player we are asked to break the record. How is it a different aspect?
2. Sometimes when we cross the limit and luck favours, we become successful. When should we cross the limit?
3. If we will not cross our limit and not go for out of box thinking, how can we get success? Give pros and cons for the same.

Day 30

Depression

Dear Children,

Depression is quiet a familiar word. It is growing exponentially. After COVID-19, many children are in its grip. Broken family bonds, westernized thoughts, endless desires, cut throat competition, living style, Junk food, poor sleeping patterns and lot of other direct and indirect reasons are responsible for causing depression. Everyone around is dissatisfied if not depressed. Dissatisfaction leads to depression if left unmonitored. These days depression is prevalent in most of the teenagers, earlier we used to observe this in old age. Loneliness of a person after the death of his/her spouse was the cause of depression, but now 50% of the world's population is suffering from this disease, however the degree may vary. Without going into details, I would like to go for the remedial measures with special emphasis on the teenagers and would like to go for the solutions only.

How will you come to know that depression is gripping you and you are having symptoms of depression? This is the question of highest order as in most of the cases, you do not accept that you are under depression. Here is a checklist:

1. When most of the time you have mood swings and are unable to tolerate even a small difference of opinion between you and your friend.
2. When you start feeling that your parents are not understanding you and always nagging you and interfering in your personal life.
3. When you lose your self-confidence and declare without any effort "I cannot do" or " I quit"

180

4. When you feel threat of every normal event, may be exam or any other event of your day to day life.
5. When there is change in your sleeping hours, either less or more than normal and the same goes with your eating habits. (Either you start eating more than usual or you lose your appetite)
6. When your social life gets disturbed, you like to be alone and avoid any company.
7. When you start procrastinating your work until it becomes urgent.
8. When you start seeing negativity everywhere, this takes one in to depression.
9. When you start doubting every other individual and feel lonely whenever the things do not go according to you.
10. When you start praying God for another COVID-19 because you want whole world to be in panic, as you feel jealous of others who are enjoying life to the fullest.
11. When tears are at the tip of your eyes ready to come out easily without any reason.

Now once you realize and accept that yes, I am under the grip of depression and 50% of the above symptoms match, you need to take it seriously and do the needful. Here are some tips, I am sharing with you.

1. Look for someone whom you can trust and who is wiser enough to pacify whenever you share your problem or wrong doing with the person.
2. Avoid bad company and start reading good books. The autobiography of the person, who had faced problems but ultimately, achieved success.
3. You need not feel guilty of your wrong doing as you are not the only one who has committed mistakes, there are many

more people. It is part of the game. Past is Past, future is uncertain, so it is better to live in present.

4. Keep yourself busy as an empty mind is a devil's workshop. Whenever you feel that there is no work, you can meditate and if you have more than 2 hours, read a good book or can watch any comedy movie.

5. Do the SWOT analysis and note down all your threats on a piece of paper. Take every threat one by one. If there is any solution, go for the same. Check the probability of the expected threat, if it is less than 5%. You may ignore it. Take each threat one by one. Cut the threat from piece of paper as well as from your heart too. Go to the next threat, repeat the exercise. Control whatever is possible and pray to God, surrender your problem to HIM but honestly. Finish till end. However, you can take a deep breath and little strolling if you feel pressure but try to complete this exercise. Writing threats and then deleting the threats with your own pen will give you relief.

6. Now take out the opportunity, you have. Who is there to help you? What is still possible? Scope of fighting back. Who is stopping you?

7. God has not created any carbon copy. Don't compare yourself with others. You are not to compete with others, you are to compete with yourself only. Sometimes When you start comparing yourself with others and sort of inferiority complex develops inside you. You may be better somewhere else. You are playing your own role and not to get depressed.

8. Sometimes there is fight between your mind and your body as your heart starts sinking and you feel helpless. You need not to wait. Consult doctor and do as per his advice. Take prescribed medicine along with fighting skill. You are to come out as a warrior.

9. Stop thinking, if someone will come to know that you are under depression, people will laugh at you. Like other disease depression is another disease and we are to take care and use our favorite mantra, I.e. Follow the master, face the devil, fight till end and finish the game.

Once you ignore and not follow the advice and will accept mood swings as natural, you will start asking questions and will blame circumstances and other factors that you are facing. Someone else is responsible for your present status. Astrologically your planetary position is unfavorable, your parents need to change their attitude and your teacher is biased with you. Your friends are selfish and you will find n number of excuses for your present status. It is going to aggravate the situation only. Don't hand over your remote control to someone else. No one will change, it is your problem and you have to change your vision. You have to do your SWOT analysis. You have already seen your threats and opportunities, now devote a day for your strengths and weaknesses too, but not verbally. Write your strengths and weaknesses and check how your strengths will help you in overcoming your weaknesses. Finally make a resolution. Write the resolution on a piece of paper in bold letters. Hang it on the wall of your bed room. Read it on a daily basis. Adhere to your own set goals and do not quit for any reason. Reaffirm your faith. Plan again and introspect, what has triggered? Why could you not manage your own set Goal?

When you continuously ignore whatever is going on and you let it proceed with a notion" I am a poor fellow and cannot fight with my circumstances and it is beyond my domain". This is the stage of deep depression and worrisome part of this stage is that some of the teenagers start thinking of ending their own lives. They feel that by ending their life they will get rid of all the existing problems and Suicide is the only solution left, they cannot even imagine what they are doing. The punishment is severest because you are not going to reach back to your destination (if you believe in rebirth). Your entry date and time to other loka is fixed and till then you will be waiting for your turn without food and sleep because you will not have the sense organ to entertain. Your soul will feel the hunger, but your body will not be there, imagine how painful it would be. You will be unable to communicate your condition to anyone else and there won't be any chance to revert back to your decision. Once you sit and count your blessings. (if you are reading this book, you are among the 5% of the world's population). You will find that there is no problem which comes without a solution. Trust, have patience and perseverance as problems are passing clouds. Tell yourself again and again" this too shall pass."

Assets :
Inquisitive Questions:
1. What do you know about stress? Is it always negative?
2. Have you ever seen someone nearby you who is under depression?
3. Which part of your body gets affected by the depression?

Suggested Activities:
Write all the blessings that God has given you as a gift.
Write your action plan in advance that you would like to do to prevent yourself from Depression.
Value Content:
Offering gratitude to God for all your blessings makes you a positive thinker. We need to appreciate others as it is going to multiply love in you.

Interesting Aside:
Sharing an experiment conducted on rats. Rats were taken and equal numbers of rats were distributed in three different cages. Two cages were having current, only difference was that there were multiple knobs in one cage to stop the current, while in second cage there was only one knob and third cage was current free. After a fixed period all the rats were taken out. Depression level of the rats with multiple knobs was more but interesting part was that depression level of the cage where there was no current was second and depression level of the rats with one knob was third. Showing that little bit effort to stop the negative situation is required.

Day to Day Relevance:
If you keep a car at rest for months, it is going to create problem, once you start using it again. Similarly, a person with zero stress too can go for depression. This phenomenon is common in USA.

Questions to Assess:
1. How far do you agree that love is undercurrent of all the values and how it helps us in reducing Depression?
2. Can a positive thinker, who believes that whatever God will give (Punishment or reward) will be for my own benefit, go for Depression?
3. Why seeing the person in pains helps you in reducing Depression (HOT)
4. Stress is necessary Evil. Elaborate. (HOT)

FEEDBACK

We hope that you would have enjoyed these lessons of Counselling. Please share your genuine feedback by rating each Chapter on a scale of 0 to 5 (0 meaning Poor and 5 meaning Excellent). You may tick below on your rating, take a picture of this page and Whatsapp on **+918146668627**.

Chapter 00: Guidelines for the Teachers	0	1	2	3	4	5
Chapter 01: The Beginning	0	1	2	3	4	5
Chapter 02: Intelligence	0	1	2	3	4	5
Chapter 03: Magic Formula of 5D	0	1	2	3	4	5
Chapter 04: 4 Formulae (4F)	0	1	2	3	4	5
Chapter 05: The Mind	0	1	2	3	4	5
Chapter 06: Meditation	0	1	2	3	4	5
Chapter 07: More of Meditation	0	1	2	3	4	5
Chapter 08: Anger Management	0	1	2	3	4	5
Chapter 09: Power of Prayer	0	1	2	3	4	5
Chapter 10: Gayatri Mantra	0	1	2	3	4	5
Chapter 11: Namasamrna	0	1	2	3	4	5
Chapter 12: Contentment	0	1	2	3	4	5
Chapter 13: Peace Of Mind	0	1	2	3	4	5
Chapter 14: Love of God, Fear of Sin & Respect	0	1	2	3	4	5
Chapter 15: Harmony Of Thoughts, Words & Deeds	0	1	2	3	4	5
Chapter 16: Time Management	0	1	2	3	4	5
Chapter 17: Values	0	1	2	3	4	5
Chapter 18: Personality	0	1	2	3	4	5
Chapter 19: Health Is Wealth	0	1	2	3	4	5
Chapter 20: Unity In Diversity	0	1	2	3	4	5
Chapter 21: Purpose of Life	0	1	2	3	4	5
Chapter 22: SWOT Analysis	0	1	2	3	4	5
Chapter 23: Law Of Karma	0	1	2	3	4	5
Chapter 24: Gratitude	0	1	2	3	4	5
Chapter 25: Stress Management	0	1	2	3	4	5
Chapter 26: Change Management	0	1	2	3	4	5
Chapter 27: Go Green	0	1	2	3	4	5
Chapter 28: Life is a Game, Play it	0	1	2	3	4	5
Chapter 29: When you cross the Limit	0	1	2	3	4	5
Chapter 30: Depression	0	1	2	3	4	5

Name: .... E-Mail Id: .... Mobile No.: ....